ELITE
MINDS

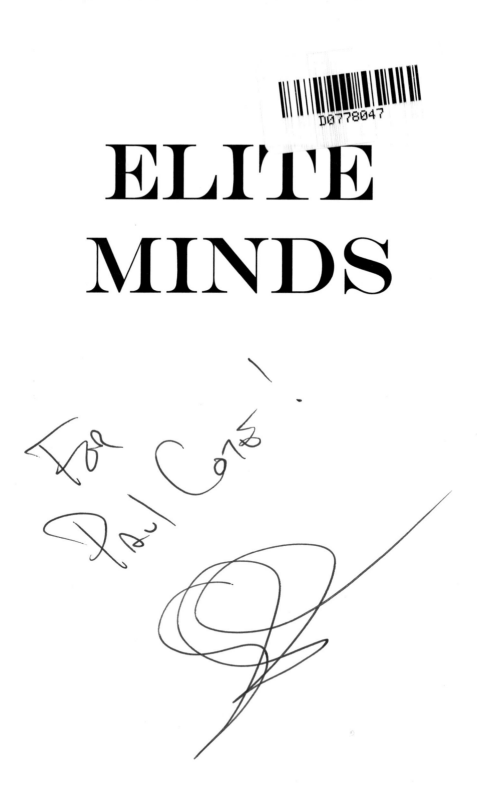

For Paul Corso!

ELITE MINDS

Creating the Competitive Advantage

Dr. Stan Beecham

*BOOK*LOGIX®
Alpharetta, Georgia

ISBN: 978-1-61005-349-5
Library of Congress Control Number: 2013911301

Printed in the United States of America

10 9 8 7 6 5 4 3 2   0 7 2 3 1 3

∞This paper meets the requirements of ANSI/NISO Z39.48-1992 (Permanence of Paper)

Author Photo by: Daniel Bianchetta

DISCLAIMER

Do not read this book if you are looking for a quick fix, motivation or just want to feel better. There is no such thing. Happy is for children. Being happy is not the purpose of your life. Being fully alive and awake is the purpose of your life. That includes the pain and struggle that is a critical and necessary component to human existence.

There are no 7 Habits, 15 Characteristics, or 21 Laws. There are No Secrets or Promises. If you desire a book that shows you the precise steps to a successful outcome, may I recommend a good cookbook; Julia Child's to be specific. However, I can promise you that your casserole will not turn out like hers, even if you do exactly what she suggests, in the exact order she recommends. Life is the same way. We think that by following someone else's recipe we will reach our destination. No, you will reach *their* destination, which will, in turn, mean you are still lost.

If you haven't bought the book yet, put it down and go back to the magazines, they will make you happy and distract you from waking the hell up and getting on with it (especially the ones with lots of pictures). That will make your friends, family, competitors and enemies very happy.

If you are still reading, good—there is hope for you. However, reading this book will likely make you feel worse not better. But hey, you were not born to be content, you were born to be complete (that's what the word "perfect" means), to be the greatest "you" possible—and the fact of the matter is, very few make it. That journey involves giving up the hope that someone else is going to give you the answer or set a plan for you that will fulfill your life long dreams. Anyone who has the audacity to suggest that others follow their path because in the eyes of the world they have been deemed successful is simply practicing narcissism. What I have attempted to do with this book is share with you my observations of people who have successfully navigated from Point A to Point B in as straight a line as possible for a human to maneuver. They have performed at the highest of levels possible—not because they followed someone else's advice, but because they had the courage to take their own.

THIS BOOK IS DEDICATED TO
ALL WHO WISH TO FLY.

In a sky full of people, only some want to fly,
isn't that crazy?

– "Crazy" by Seal, 1990

CONTENTS

FOREWORD

In August 1996, I walked onto the University of Georgia campus ready to play collegiate golf for one of the most decorated women's golf programs in the country. I was internally motivated by my goals of gaining an education while hoping to equip myself with the tools to take my game to an even higher level. As a student-athlete, I wanted to use all of my resources to help me achieve my goals of one day playing on the Ladies Professional Golf Tour (LPGA). I had always lived by the quote, "Champions are made, not born!" I was motivated to be great!

Beans Kelly, my head coach at the University of Georgia, called a team meeting one August afternoon at the beginning of our fall season. It was a group session to start some work with our athletic department's sport psychologist. I will never forget that moment when Dr. Stan Beecham entered the room to start his lesson on team cohesion and personal beliefs. I was intrigued by what he said that day. Dr. Beecham lit a fire in me to become curious about my golf game and myself. He made me ask myself the question, "What is missing inside of me that might be holding me back?" I wanted to explore this question even further, but was frightened by what I might find out about myself. Dr. Beecham could sense that my wheels were turning and I was hungry to learn more. From that first encounter in fall semester, my life was forever changed. I knew I was good at the game of golf, but he helped me cultivate a plan to become great!

Dr. Beecham asked me the tough questions and forced me to face my biggest fears. By facing those fears, I was able to free up my mind to play golf in a way that I had never dreamed would be possible. We had weekly meetings and worked consistently on creating a system of beliefs about myself that led to some amazing results both on and off the golf course.

Creating a consistent discipline to train my mind daily to believe that I belonged at the top allowed me to perform at the highest level week in and week out. I became a four-time All-American, Southeastern Conference Freshman of the Year, two-time Southeastern Conference Player of the Year, and numerous individual and team titles were added to my resume. Dr. Beecham convinced me to believe that winning was a habit and that mental focus and practice was more important than my technical training.

I always knew that college was a stepping-stone for my future life and would give me the tools to face the real world after graduation. Dr. Beecham helped me transform my inner self to a place that I am proud to stand today.

Due to an early diagnosis of Rheumatoid Arthritis, my professional golf career was cut short. Fortunately, I was able to stay in the game of golf as the head women's golf coach at The University of Arkansas. Dr. Beecham has remained a huge resource even to this day as I work tirelessly to provide a mental toughness and competitive environment that allows my teams to compete at the highest level. He continues to make me hungry to reach outside of my boundaries and to think consistently outside of the box. As humans, we are often uncomfortable being different or not doing the norm, but the thing I love most about my time with Dr. Beecham is his constant prodding and a persistence to try the impossible.

I admire Dr. Beecham for finally reaching out and doing what he thought was impossible by writing this book. *Elite Minds* is a window into his spirit and into his unique perspective on how to out-think the competition. I have been blessed to learn about this for over fifteen years now. It will challenge you to take a risk and to look at things differently. It is a great lesson on gratitude and setting an intention for a journey. I hope his words inspire you as much as they have forever changed me as a person and a coach.

Shauna Estes-Taylor
University of Arkansas Head Women's Golf Coach
Inductee: NGCA Players Hall of Fame

PREFACE

There is but one cause of human failure.
And that is man's lack of faith in his true Self.

– William James

He is able who thinks he is able.

– Buddha

Years ago, I was working with some Olympic-level gymnasts in Cincinnati. The coach would have me come up for a weekend once a month. The elite girls would work out in the morning and again in the afternoons, but the rest of the time there wasn't much for me to do. We decided that one evening, while the younger kids were training, I would meet with the parents to talk about how to support kids who wanted to become great gymnasts like the Olympic-level girls who trained earlier in the day.

The presentation began with a simple question: *What is the job of a parent?* How would you know if you did a good job parenting or if you had failed your kid? Though they each phrased it differently, the typical response was something about having happy, content kids who generally enjoy their lives.

I disagreed with the notion that successful parenting is about happy kids and suggested to the parents that instead, their primary job was to prepare their children to live independently. In effect, to put themselves out of business and render their roles obsolete.

It wasn't exactly what they wanted to hear.

The idea of your child not needing you anymore is a troubling thought to most parents. But, ultimately, to hold them back is to keep them from reaching their full potential. They will learn, one way or another, how to get along as adults in the world. The real question is: *how* will they learn? Alone, in the school of hard knocks? Or, together, with an adult who can help them avoid the major pitfalls?

Do you remember the story of Icarus? In Greek mythology, Icarus and his father, Daedalus, were held prisoners on Crete, imprisoned in the labyrinth that his father had built to contain the Minotaur. Daedalus, an inventor and master craftsman, built two pair of wings out of wax and feathers for both of them to escape the island prison.

Daedalus warned Icarus not to fly too high because the sun would melt the wax and not to fly too low for the sea would make the feathers wet and heavy. But when Icarus took off, he was overcome with the thrill of flying and flew too close to the sun. The wax melted and he crashed into the sea and died.

Most people see this story as a lesson in naïve ambition. I see it as a warning of what will ultimately happen if we try to imprison or hold someone back from being free.

Think about it: Icarus was wrongfully imprisoned and risked his life to be free. He escaped by taking a huge risk and trying something that had never been done before. What if his only problem is that he was never taught to fly? What if his father's fear, not his own, put him in a perilous situation?

Most of us are Daedalus, and our dreams for life are like Icarus—fearless and adventurous, but endangered by the chains of fear.

Fear of loss and failure is what keeps you from reaching your potential and it is the same poison that leads you to discourage others—often unconsciously—from reaching their full potential. But the lesson we all need to internalize is that it's not an either/or world. You are not a winner *or* a loser, a success *or* a failure. You are and forever will be both. And it is our failure to accept that we are both that seems to be the primary impediment to our growth.

The truth is, there are no magic habits, traits, or characteristics. No one side has all the right answers, and I most certainly have much to learn. This book is simply an attempt to help you discover a way to tell yourself the truth about what you are and what you are not.

To think of oneself as either a winner or a loser is to live a lie. Success is not the avoidance of failure any more than life is the avoidance of death. We *need* failure and loss. Our life and our development depend upon it. Life and competition make no sense and have no purpose without both success and failure, yet we are constantly troubled by and suffer as a result of our failures because we do not believe that failure is essential to our growth.

This is the age in which every child is special, every athlete is awarded a trophy for donning the uniform, and no child is left behind. It sends the wrong message. Our primary challenge is that we must first quit lying to ourselves and then stop lying to one another.

You and I have both failed and we will fail again. We know this to be true. And the truth is true whether we believe it or not.

However, we also know that we are not failures. If you have made it to adulthood and still have your sanity, then you have learned to some degree how to make sense of the simple fact that you are both wonderful and terrible, a winner and a loser, a success and a failure. It is within this tension, this struggle, that we live what we call a "life."

This book is intended to help you make sense of your failures, not eliminate them. I want you to have more successes, to reach your potential—but not in the "blow sunshine up your skirt" kind of way. For this reason, these pages don't offer my twenty-five tricks to being successful every day of your life and never feeling bad about yourself again. As a psychologist specializing in high performance, I know that struggle, suffering, and pain are what makes our lives so damn interesting and our endeavors so damn exciting. Let's not wish that away, but let's learn to make sense of it so that we don't all have to take Xanax or drink a bottle of whiskey in order to make peace with ourselves.

Like the Buddha said, we suffer because we want our situation to be different, not because of the situation. Your failures are so painful in part because you think you must not fail in order to be okay. It's why you shrink back in fear. Let's make the decision right now to forget that line of thinking. Failure isn't fun; but it is a very necessary part of your success. And not just your success; everyone's success.

During the many encounters I've shared with elite athletes and executives, I usually come away thinking how normal and ordinary they are. They were not levitating several inches above the ground, nor did they seem to go through life avoiding all the pitfalls. They all persevered through pain, sometimes unthinkable pain. They all grieved and kept going. They all breathed in and then breathed out.

They all stumbled and fell. They all failed and struggled with frustration, anxiety, and fear. Just like you and me.

In fact, on the outside, their lives appeared pretty much the same as yours and mine. The difference was on the inside. What set them apart was how they internally processed their lives—both failures and successes—and learned to believe the truth about how high they could fly. They developed what I like to call, "elite minds."

In the pages to come, I'll do my best to show you precisely what that means by allowing you to peer through the lens I've been given over the last two decades. I believe this is the most effective way for you to see how you can develop your own elite mind.

Stan Beecham
Roswell, Georgia,
2013

ACKNOWLEDGMENTS

All human actions have one or all of these seven causes:
chance, nature, compulsion, habit, reason, passion and desire.

– Aristotle

As you will read later in this book, I don't believe in the concept of individual performance. In other words, no one has ever done anything on his or her own. We all need help, and I have been the recipient of a tremendous amount of help while writing this book.

First, I want to give a shout out to my family. My parents, Paul and Sara Beecham, did a wonderful job of giving my brother, Steve, and I a lot of independence and encouragement to fly. They understood the world is in fact a classroom and the best way to learn is to do.

My family, Judy, Kate and Will, they take nothing at face value and have challenged me to become a better father and man. I am lucky to be on their team.

Scott Humphrey works for one of my biggest clients, Shaw Industries, in Dalton, Georgia. Scott has given me the opportunity to speak to both Shaw employees and their customers many times over the years. Several years ago, he began to ask me when I was going to write a book. Every time I would speak at Shaw, Scott would ask me when the book would be ready. Everyone needs a Scott in their life to both encourage and challenge them.

Vince Dooley said "yes" to me in 1994, when he could have very easily said "no." If you are competent, all you need is for someone to give you a chance. When Coach Dooley gave me the chance to start a sport psychology program at the University of Georgia, I wasn't even competent.

My four years at UGA were wonderful, thanks in part to the great coaches who supported and trusted me with their athletes including Jack Baurle, Harvey Humphries, Jeff Wallace, Suzanne Yoculan, Hugh Durham, Tubby Smith, Andy Landers, John Mitchell, Wayne McDuffie, Chris Haack, Manny Diaz, and Beans Kelly. I learned so much from my time with you all.

Pete Rea and Greg McMillan coach some of the best distance runners in America. They have given me the opportunity to work with and learn from their athletes. I am grateful to you both.

There have been a number of companies that have allowed me to feed my family by talking to their employees. I am especially grateful to Shaw Industries in Dalton, Georgia; TXU Energy in Dallas, Texas; Loretta Cecil and McKesson in Alpharetta, Georgia; Dupont in Athens, Georgia; Charlie Merinoff and Charmer-Sunbelt Industries in New York.

I also want to thank Shauna Estes-Taylor, the head coach of the women's golf team at the University of Arkansas, who is still one of the best competitors I have ever known. We worked together when she was a four-time All American golfer at the University of Georgia.

And finally, I must thank Scotty Fletcher Brewington, Brent Cole, and Caroline Donahue, my editors. You have probably heard the ancient Chinese parable, "When the student is ready, the teacher will come." Well, for me it was, "When the writer is ready, the editors will come." Thanks for coming at the perfect time.

INTRODUCTION
The Beginning

Children usually do not blame themselves for getting lost.

– Anna Freud

Knowledge rests not upon truth alone, but upon error also.

– Carl Jung

My interest in sport psychology began out of my own experiences as an athlete. Like most boys, I dreamed of playing ball my entire life. That didn't happen. What did was that I learned first-hand how poorly prepared I was to compete on any level, let alone an elite one.

When I was growing up, most coaches knew very little about the mental aspect of sports and how to train athletes to be true competitors. Looking back, I realize that had I been in a different environment, I would have performed at a much higher level. (This is true for the vast majority of athletes). For this realization, I largely have Tommy Friedman, my ninth grade football coach, to thank.

During seventh and eighth grade, I played football for the local community team. I was a pretty good athlete and played both defensive and offensive line. Yet, when it came time to sign up for my ninth grade year, I decided I didn't want to play anymore. I had lost the joy of competing.

In hindsight, I attribute this to the grown-ups in charge at the time— the coaches. Their inability to have fun had trickled down to us kids. Even though I found the games on Saturday to be a total blast, I just couldn't stomach the grueling Monday through Friday practice schedule. It was monotonous and tiresome and often left me with a headache.

Tommy Friedman was the owner of the local hobby shop and father of one of my friends, Ben, who I had played ball with in the past. One Friday night I ran into him at the local high school football game.

"Stan, are you going to play football this year?" he asked. Because he was the coach and had the roster, he already knew I had not signed up.

"No sir, I'm not going to play football anymore," I told him.

"Why? You were one of the best guys on the team last year. We need you!"

"I just don't want to play," I confessed. "It's just not fun anymore."

"I completely understand. I have been watching you boys for the last couple of years and I decided to coach this year because I think it *should* be fun. I really want you to come out and play."

Then Tommy Friedman did something no other coach had ever done before or since. He made me a promise. "Stan," he said, "I'll make a deal with you. Come out and join us for the first few practices and I guarantee you, we will have lots of fun. If we don't, you can quit and I will not be mad at you or try to make you stay. Do we have a deal?"

It was an offer—and a promise—I couldn't refuse. We shook hands. The fact of the matter is: I wanted to play. I just didn't want to hate the sport five days a week so that I could love it on Saturday.

How do you think our team of eighth and ninth graders did that year? I'll give you a hint: Tommy Friedman kept his word and it was the most fun I ever had playing ball. We won more games than any team from Roswell, Georgia, ever had. We beat teams no team from Roswell had ever beaten. We even made it to the playoffs, and while we eventually lost before reaching the championship, it was a season, a team, and an experience I'll never forget.

Now, thirty-five years later, I still remember how we ended practice most days. Tommy would call us all in after we had run sprints. He would say, "Men, come in real close. There are lots of mothers standing by the fence and I don't want them to hear me."

For the next five minutes, Tommy would tell us the dirty jokes that salesmen had told him that week in his store. We left practice every day laughing. One evening, as I got in the car with my mother, she asked, "What is Tommy saying to you boys at the end of practice—is he using profanity?"

"No, Mom. He's just telling us about the other team and how we are going to beat them."

The lesson I learned in the ninth grade that many coaches still miss today is that every athlete wants to enjoy playing the game and, ultimately, to enjoy the struggle of getting better.

Fast forward a few years. During my undergraduate years at the University of Georgia (1979–1983), I began to study the psychology of sport. It was a relatively new field and there were a couple of journals about it in the school library. Hungry to learn, I read them all.

The journal articles were mostly about very basic tenets such as internal imagery, goal setting, and positive self-talk. Once you had read one article on the topic, there wasn't much more new information. I kept reading, anyway, in the hope that something new and exciting would appear. It rarely did. But the constant reading did provide me with enough naïve confidence that I could now go out and apply these insights in the real world.

Kevin Butler was the placekicker for Georgia at the time and I knew him because he dated a friend of mine named Cathy who eventually became his wife. I shared with Kevin some of the things I had learned, most of it around the concept of mental practice and rehearsal.

Kevin, being a nice guy and very interested in how to improve, wanted to work with me. All I had to do then was convince the head football coach, Vince Dooley, to let me come out on the field during practice and work with his kicker.

Kevin got me an audience with Coach Dooley who told me to come out to practice that spring to discuss the matter. I was a twenty-year-old kid who didn't know what the hell I was doing but I was dumb enough to think I did. So at an opportune moment during the first day of spring practice, a couple of years after Georgia won the National Championship on the legs of Herschel Walker, I approached one of the legendary coaches of college football and suggested that he let me work with the best placekicker in all of college football, who, by the way, is to this day the *only* placekicker to ever be selected into the College Football Hall of Fame.

Coach Dooley had no reason to say yes. He should have said, "Kid, seriously. You think you can help one of the best kickers in the history of the game because you read a bunch of journals in the basement of the library? Are you kidding me?" But he didn't. He listened to me then looked at me and just said, "Okay." That's when the trajectory of my life expanded immensely.

I came back to UGA the following fall to work with Kevin and the other kickers. It was an incredible experience. Looking back, I realize Kevin and Coach Dooley both took a big chance letting me work with them. Who knows if I did any good, but I sure didn't make things worse. Georgia had a good season, beat Texas in the Cotton Bowl, and one highlight of the year was when Kevin kicked a 60-yard field goal in the final seconds to win the game against Clemson. In a small way, I felt that the accomplishment was something I could be proud of, too.

During the mid-1980's, I attended a graduate program in psychology at Augusta College. My interest in sports was still there, but I had nowhere to direct my energy. Reading the journals, I learned that there was a sport psychology convention in Hilton Head, South Carolina, which was only a few hours' drive from Augusta. Even though I didn't have the money to pay the conference fee, I decided to go anyway and just see what it was all about.

Bob Rotella was a professor at the University of Virginia at the time and he had become a very well-known sport psychologist. He had written a few articles that I really enjoyed and was one of the few sport psychology guys who was actually working with athletes (most were professors who mainly did research and taught).

I met Rotella at the conference and introduced myself, telling him about my desire to one day do what he was doing. That was probably the tenth time he had heard the line that day, but he was kind and heard me out. He then suggested I not attend a sport psychology program, but try to get into a clinical or counseling psychology program instead. He knew there were very few jobs in the sports field and that was not likely to change any time soon. I thanked him, snuck into a few sessions at the conference, and headed back to Augusta to follow his advice.

By 1993, I had just completed my doctoral training in clinical psychology and was jumping over the last hurdle of a doctorate program. A yearlong internship at the University of Virginia Counseling Center was all that stood between me and my freedom to go out and finally make a living.

While at Virginia, I looked up Bob Rotella again and reminded him of our conversation six years earlier. At the time, Rotella was still teaching at Virginia and working with quite a few PGA touring pros. He agreed to allow me to sit in on a graduate seminar class he was teaching.

Rotella has an amazing ability to convince you that you really can get what you want if you are willing to earn it. During that class, I realized that my dream was to return to UGA and start a sport psychology program for the athletic program. Fortunately, Vince Dooley said okay again and in 1994, I moved back to Athens to start the program. The experience that ensued signified the beginning of the lessons that would eventually lead to the overarching message of this book: when you truly study top performers in any field, what sets them apart is not their physical skill; it is how they control their minds. Top performers have mastered how to think and what to believe in order to maximize what they do—their performance—

again and again. And they provide you and me with a clear path for taking our performances to their highest level.

Here's where that begins.

1

PHYSICALITY VS. MENTALITY

If you plan on being anything less than you are capable of being you will probably be unhappy all the days of your life.

– Abraham Maslow

The debate continues, whether it's in business or competitive sport: How much of one's performance is based on physical ability, and how much of one's performance is based on mental acuity? Perhaps Yogi Bera said it best when he explained, "Baseball is ninety-percent mental, and the other half is physical." From where I sit, the view's a little different. I believe the degree to which one performs and the level of success one achieves is 100 percent mental.

Why?

Because the mind is in control of the body.

This is not my opinion—it is scientifically verified by those who have studied the brain/mind complex for decades. Your brain is the software; your body the hardware. Simply put, your body does what your brain tells it to do, or what your brain thinks your body is capable of doing.

Misunderstandings about the keys to performance exist because we have a bias towards the physical. In predicting success today, both coaches and business leaders are drunk on the elixir of talent and experience. We believe that if you can find a talented person who has matured with experience, then you should select that person for your team.

Sport is more swayed by talent, and business more so by experience, but they both look to those two attributes as the primary determinates of success. Unfortunately, it's not the best way to go about it. In fact, talent and experience alone will never lead to a sustained high-level of performance—especially at the elite level in any given field.

The problem with this approach is that *everyone* is talented and has years of experience at the elite level. Who then performs the best when the advantage of talent and experience are mitigated?

The answer is simple: the person whose mind is an asset, not an obstruction.

The competitive advantage at the highest level is overwhelmingly mental, not physical.

I see this every day.

There are thousands of talented kids in college who never make it in the pros, and there are extremely bright and knowledgeable managers who fail to advance beyond the director or vice president level. These are the people I am frequently called in to work with. In a corporate setting, the conversation usually begins like this:

"Dr. Stan, we have this manager who is very bright and talented but is struggling to get her team performing at the level we need them to be. She has a great education and has worked at some of the best companies in our industry, but she is not having the impact we expected."

In a sports setting, coaches usually talk in terms of an athlete not reaching his or her *full potential*:

"The kid's got raw talent. He even looks great in practice and at times makes it look effortless. But when I put him in the game, he's a totally different person."

A similar phenomenon is found in schools, where we observe smart kids who are unable to process information when taking a test. We call it "test anxiety" and shake our heads.

Before I further explain how such underachievement occurs, let's make some terms clear from the get-go so there is no confusion when we talk about the relationship between our minds and our performance.

To begin, what you need to know about your operating system— the brain—is that the way in which the brain functions is referred to as *the mind*. You can see a brain, but you can't see a mind.

The mind is thus divided into two major categories: the conscious and the unconscious. The *conscious* mind is the part of your brain you are aware of. This is where you think, plan, solve problems, and experience emotions. The *unconscious* mind is a powerful determinate of behavior. It houses what you believe, the things you hold as truth. Unfortunately, most people are unaware of their unconscious mind and the beliefs they hold to be true. Typically, while we are keenly aware of what we think and feel (conscious), the majority of us have very little understanding of what we really believe about ourselves and the world around us (unconscious). And this is where performance shortcomings arise.

What you believe about yourself and your world is the primary determinant to what you do and, ultimately, how well you do it.

This is not a new idea. While Sigmund Freud still catches a lot of grief for his psychosexual hypotheses, he ultimately made a name for himself by bringing the unconscious mind to the forefront of psychology. To understand how this came about, you should know that Freud did not begin as a psychologist. While he became one, Freud actually began as a neurologist, studying such diseases as cerebral palsy and other neuromuscular disorders.

Patients would come to Freud with tangible physical defects and limitations. Much to his own surprise, Freud was frequently unable to find any physical cause for the patient's paralysis, blindness, or pain. There was simply no physical explanation for the symptoms the patients exhibited.

Fortunately for us, Freud was a very curious and brilliant man who was unwilling to settle for a simple, "I'm sorry your arm is paralyzed, but I can't help you" response. Instead, Freud stayed at it and began to talk to patients about the other things happening in their lives. This is where he struck gold.

Freud soon realized that the cause of many disorders was not physical, but mental. Often, the patient's *mind* was the problem. The unconscious mind was causing the body to fail to perform properly. Back in Freud's day, this groundbreaking discovery was at first scorned by the entire medical community. Today, the mind-body relationship is widely accepted as ailments like stress and anxiety remain leading causes of health issues nationwide, not to mention leading causes of sudden drops in performance—whether on the ball field or in the boardroom. Unfortunately, the medical and athletic communities aren't completely sold on the power of the mind. I'd be lying if I said I thought the medical and fitness communities are doing anything more than paying lip service to this most important of issues—the unconscious mind/body connection.

The truth is that we still prefer to initiate performance improvement and longevity from a tangible standpoint, and then look at other alternative options if that doesn't work. While approaches like surgery, physical therapy, physical training regimens, and diets certainly hold their value and always will, we will continually fail to reach performance goals until we learn to utilize the engine of our minds.

Years ago, I attended a sport psychology conference where I noticed on the calendar that a prominent orthopedic surgeon, Dr. Richard Steadman, would be speaking that day. Steadman had operated on many great athletes. (If you remember, Kobe Bryant was getting his knee worked on by Steadman when he made headlines in Colorado.) At first, I was curious as to why a surgeon would be speaking at a sport psychology conference, but given the options during that hour, he seemed like the most interesting choice.

What Dr. Steadman said that day has never left my mind. Dr. Steadman acknowledged how modern medicine has thoroughly researched and documented the role stress and other mental maladies play in the onset of disease and illness. He was there that day not only to validate modern medicine's findings, but also to take them a step further. He was there to share his belief that there is a relationship between one's mental state and accidental injury.

Steadman explained that when he would meet a new patient for the first time, he would ask them a simple question: "What happened?" Over the years, he began to notice that people were less prone to give him *physical* reasons for the accident, and more likely to offer him *psychological* explanations for how they became injured.

He heard less, "I was skiing along and hit a patch of ice that caused me to fall and my leg bent backwards. That's when I heard a pop." Instead, his patients' explanations were more often along the lines of, "My wife and I were arguing because I wanted to hit the slopes and she wanted me to wait another thirty minutes for her to get ready. I told her I was going to make one quick run and then meet her at Lionshead in one hour. So, I hurried up the mountain and flew down the hill to make sure I met her on time and that's when I fell awkwardly and heard a pop."

Keep in mind, Dr. Steadman is not some peripheral quack who is talking to sport psychologists because he has lost the respect of his peers. He is one of the leading doctors in his field. You don't make an appointment with him; you request one. If you need knee surgery, there are only a handful of elite options, and he is one of them.

His message to us that day was that accidents don't just *happen*. There are psychological antecedents to all human behavior, even accidents. In other words, every physical event is preceded by a psychological event. Could it be true? I believe so; and in the pages that follow, I'll explain precisely why. For now, let me continue setting the stage with a few more thought-provoking examples from my own experience.

One of the most interesting conversations I ever had with a coach was with Tubby Smith, the former basketball coach at the University of Georgia, while we were both getting dressed in the men's locker room. I had noticed that his athletes were not getting injured at the same rate as athletes on other teams. I asked Tubby why he thought this was true.

His reply was simple and precise, "I tell my team we are not going to get injured. We will do the things we need to do to prevent injury, and we will warm up before practice and do some exercises to keep us strong, but we will simply not get injured."

Tubby clearly understood what very few other coaches do—that injury rate is closely correlated with a belief system. Tubby believed his team was not going to get injured, and they believed what he said. Compare this to the belief system that most coaches have. How many times have you heard a coach say, "Injury is unfortunately just a part of the game…You enter every season knowing that some athletes will get hurt…It's unavoidable…You just hope the injury bug doesn't bite your key guys at important times."

Some teams have recurring problems with injuries that keep them from ever reaching their full potential. But if someone were to suggest that a large part of the cause was psychological, most coaches would just laugh at you. Unfortunately, these same coaches would miss one of the most important keys to their success.

This same dynamic is true in business. Show me the number of sick days a company has per employee and I can accurately predict the psychological health of the company culture. There is more to "accident prone" people than meets the eye.

Illness and injury are huge factors in a business' financial success as well. Some estimates suggest that approximately 50 percent of corporate profits go towards health care. American companies lose between $200–300 billion each year in stress-related illness and lost productivity.

Unscheduled absences cost employers $3,600 per hourly employee per year and $2,650 per salaried employee per year. The American Medical Association has stated that stress is the cause of 80–85 percent of all illness and disease.

Recently, I read *The Biology of Belief* by Dr. Bruce Lipton. If you are interested in digging deeper into the relationship between mind and body, you will find his book intriguing. Lipton begins one chapter with a story about a Dr. Mason, who successfully treated a fifteen-year-old boy, whom he believed had warts, with hypnosis alone. Dr. Mason had successfully treated wart patients with hypnosis in the past and had no reason to believe it would not work with this patient. However, the boy didn't actually have warts. Mason just thought he did. The truth was that he had a far more serious and potentially deadly skin disease known as congenital ichthyosis, a disease that makes the skin leathery.

The fact that Dr. Mason successfully treated the boy with only the power of the human mind shocked the medical community. More patients with skin conditions were sent to Dr. Mason, yet he was unable to cure them of their disease.

After several unsuccessful attempts, the doctor concluded why he was unable to help subsequent patients. He acknowledged that, with the successful treatment, he did not know the proper diagnosis, but truly believed he could cure the patient and the patient also believed in his treatment. However, the future treatments failed simply because he admitted that he did not believe hypnosis would succeed in treating the disorder. To that point, he had been confident he could treat warts with hypnosis. Treating anything else brought doubt into the equation. And doubt nullified the doctor's effectiveness.

This phenomenon helps explain faith healing and other primitive treatments that have documented success.

KEY TAKEAWAY

Your mind can make you sick and your mind can heal you.

Tubby Smith believed in this same approach to injury prevention and his athletes believed in him. That's why it worked. The unconscious mind, what you truly believe is true, determines what the body does and can do. The conscious mind can only sit, observe, think, and worry.

If you're still a bit skeptical of all this so-called "psychobabble," consider the following: Dr. Daniel Amen, a well-known child and adult psychiatrist who has done extensive work in evaluating psychiatric and neurological patients with the help of brain imaging, says there is nothing more important to your health and, ultimately, your life, than what you believe to be true. But the question remains: How can the mind override the body and the genetic makeup that we all inherit at birth?

The answer is found in physics.

Modern physics has demonstrated that matter and energy are the same. We think of the mind as energy and the body as matter, but quantum physics has taught us that matter is made up of energy. A piece of steel is essentially energy that is being held very tightly together.

Thoughts (the brain's energy) directly impact the physical brain, which, in turn, controls the functions of the body. Through modern science, we now know that thought-energy can activate or inhibit physical functionality on a cellular level.

Everyone who took Psychology 101 in college remembers the story of Pavlov's dog and the theory of conditioning. In short, Pavlov was studying the digestion of dogs in a laboratory. (Like Freud, he did not begin his career as a psychologist). Every day, the dogs were fed and every day, they heard the sound of a bell when their caretaker came through the door to feed them. The dogs learned to associate the sound of the bell with food. As soon as they heard the bell, they began to salivate in anticipation of food.

The take away from the research is that learning and behavioral changes can take place at an unconscious or unintentional level. Unconscious learning leads to unconscious behavioral changes, which in turn lead to the creation of unconscious habits. Most of the habitual behaviors we exhibit today were not acquired through a deliberate and intentional process. Even simple nervous habits like biting our nails or touching our faces when talking were brought about by unconscious beliefs that stem from some unconscious lesson we learned along the way.

The good news is that it is always possible to develop new habits or change old, unconscious ones through the use of the conscious mind, which is deliberate and intentional. This point is the major thrust of the book.

In fact, if I was to summarize the primary difference between elite competitors and those who are not, is that elite competitors make it their business to understand and manage their unconscious minds by mastering their conscious thoughts and behavior. Simply put, they outperform others because they have trained themselves to believe, think, and behave in optimal unison.

Most scientists who focus on the relationship between unconscious beliefs and behavior believe that the unconscious mind is in control of the human body 90–95 percent of the time. I'm not sure how one comes to such conclusions and, frankly, I don't think it matters if the unconscious mind is in control 50 percent or 95 percent of the time. The important thing to realize is that if you are in the business of changing behavior and improving performance, you must understand that your unconscious mind plays a major role in this thing we call success, performance, excellence, or greatness. And if you can learn to manage your unconscious mind, you can learn to master your performance in any physical endeavor.

KEY TAKEAWAY

Most people don't choose their habits. Successful people bring conscious thinking to a mostly unconscious process.

Now that I've demonstrated how powerful the unconscious mind is and how it tends to dominate our behavior, I want to remind you to not give up on the underdog—the conscious mind. It is also powerful and has the ability to move mountains.

Free will, drive, determination, and motivation are all byproducts of the conscious mind. The good news is that the conscious mind has the capacity to override the unconscious mind. The keyword here is "capacity." Sadly, most of us do not take advantage of this ability and instead function on autopilot.

Most of the things we learn and accept as truth take place at the unconscious level. Even if the information is false or inaccurate, it is accepted at the unconscious level as truth.

If you repeatedly tell a young child that she is smart, for example, she will believe you. How does she even know what *smart* is? She probably doesn't, but she believes she is regardless. Likewise, if a father continually tells his son that he is lazy, the son will adopt that belief of himself as well. This is what social psychologists refer to as the "Looking Glass Phenomenon." Children adopt the beliefs of their parents and other significant others because they are not born with a belief system. They adopt one. You adopted a belief system too—do you know whose belief system you adopted? If not, you have some homework to do. That begins by understanding how your current belief system came to be—most likely without you even noticing.

Your mind is incredibly fast. It processes information at a speed you cannot even imagine. Once you see an object, it takes your brain about a half-second to generate an emotional response. That's how fast the unconscious mind works. And seeing only represents one-fifth of the ways in which your brain receives information. When you also consider the constant streams of information coming from what you are hearing, tasting, touching and smelling, it's easy to see how habits are formed without a conscious thought—including habitual beliefs.

There is simply no time to use the conscious mind to think about something if the unconscious mind works that fast on that much information simultaneously. Therefore, to improve our behavior and ultimately our performance, we must get our unconscious minds wired and ready for success *before* events happen. This is where mental practice, imagery, self-talk and other techniques come into play and become very valuable tools.

Everyone practices some form of self-deception because we all believe things that are not true and yet have no idea that our belief is inaccurate. Once we internalize the belief, it becomes part of our brain's operating system, similar to how a virus infects a computer. You didn't want it and may not have known when the virus (false belief) entered the system, but now that it's in, it's very difficult to get rid of it.

KEY TAKEAWAY

We do what we think we can. We don't attempt what we think we are incapable of.

Your current performance, whether you are an employee or an athlete, is the sum of your belief system, which is subconscious (i.e. made up of beliefs you do not actively think about whether or not you know the basis of those beliefs). Great bosses and coaches affect the belief system of their subordinates via the conscious process. This, too, is where you can begin if you want to be your own best boss or coach.

My seventeen-year-old daughter, Kate, is quite a good distance runner. She knows I work with professional runners, but that doesn't get me any points with her. As the old adage goes, "No man can be a prophet in his own town." And certainly not in his own home.

However, during the cross-country season of her sophomore year, I bought her a pair of compression socks. We were driving to her race one Saturday morning and I suggested she try the socks for the first time during her race that day.

"Do you think it will help?" she asked.

"Absolutely," I said. "I bet you run at least a minute faster than you normally do if you wear the socks. Your legs will feel lighter and fresher."

Surprisingly, she took my advice and wore the socks. Not surprisingly, she ran the fastest race of her life and broke the nineteen-minute barrier in a 5K cross-country event for the first time ever. Her teammates were amazed by her improved performance and soon they all wanted to know where they could get a pair of the socks.

The following week at the next race, not only did all of the girls have on compression socks, they also bought the same brand and color. This is a powerful example of what psychologists refer to as the *placebo effect*. A placebo has no true medical, chemical or physical benefits. However, placebos are extremely effective because of the effect they have on the mind of the individual.

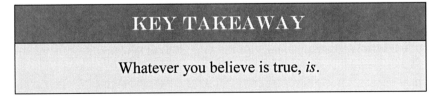

KEY TAKEAWAY

Whatever you believe is true, *is*.

Modern medicine has disassociated itself from the benefits of placebos primarily because there is not much money to be made selling sugar pills. But the placebo effect is not only observed with drugs. It is also observed with surgery.

The New England Journal of Medicine published an article in 2002 where the placebo effect was tested in surgery. The lead author noted in the article that, "All good surgeons know there is no placebo effect in surgery," yet had the courage to test that assumption.

Subjects were placed into one of three groups. Group One had the damaged cartilage in their knees shaved away. Group Two had their knee joints flushed out with a solution and tissue removed that was believed to be causing the arthritis. Both of these two surgeries were the standard treatment at the time for an arthritic knee. Group Three—the placebo group—was sedated for surgery and three small incisions were made, but no actual surgery took place.

What do you think were the results of the study? There was no significant difference between the three groups. But that's not the surprising news. What is even more amazing to me is that findings like these are all but ignored by the medical community including doctors, hospitals, insurance companies, and pharmaceutical companies. As a rule, they don't like the fact that the placebo effect is real because it's terrible for business!

It certainly got my attention, as I have had this exact surgery on both of my knees.

Think about how many products are on the market today that don't benefit the consumer one bit. Now think about how many products are on the market today that not only don't help, but are proven to do *harm* to the consumer. Last time I checked, the tobacco companies were doing just fine.

When consulting with business leaders, I remind them of the importance of communication and the words they use. If you pause to think about it, communicating is what most leaders and coaches do for a living. It is their ability to communicate that ultimately determines their success.

Science has recently demonstrated the incredible power of the spoken word. We now know that the words a person hears from his superior elicit a chemical response in the brain. The brain structure consists of brain cells (neurons) and chemicals (neurotransmitters) that bridge the gap between the neurons. These chemicals are the substances that psychotropic agents like anti-depressants and anti-anxiety drugs affect in order to elicit an emotional change in the patient.

What this means is that words have the capacity to change the chemical balance in the brain just as effectively as Prozac and Xanax, but without the negative side effects or expensive deductibles.

KEY TAKEAWAY

You can change someone's brain chemistry, emotions, and beliefs with the power of your words.

You can't talk about the placebo effect without mentioning the *nocebo* effect (the power of negative beliefs). In 1961, Walter Kennedy coined the term "nocebo," which in Latin means, "I will harm." (The term "placebo" in Latin means "I will please.") The power of the negative nocebo is just as awesome as the power of the positive placebo. Unfortunately, it appears that there is more nocebo than placebo going on these days.

In an experimental condition, the placebo and the nocebo effect can be the same. The only difference is what the doctor and patient believe the agent will elicit before the treatment phase has begun. With the placebo, the most powerful responses occur when both the doctor and patient believe the placebo will work. The same is true with the nocebo. When both parties believe something will be damaging, it usually is. (The next time you buy a voodoo doll and stick needles in it, make sure the person you are casting your spell upon knows what you are doing and believes in the ill effects of such a spell.)

Our unconscious and conscious belief systems not only affect our health, behavior, habits and performance, but also determine our quality of life. The concept of confidence has received a tremendous amount of attention in both the sports and business arenas. Confidence is just another way to describe our belief systems.

Every time I hear someone say, "I feel confident," I ask them if confidence is a feeling or a thought. Most think of it as an emotion. Confidence at an unconscious level may seem like an emotion because of the individual's sense of being controlled by the belief. However, once you become conscious of confidence, you quickly realize that confidence is a thought, not an emotion.

In order to help individuals improve their confidence, you have to work at the conscious level and address it as a thought. As long as individuals with low confidence view it as a feeling, they will never be able to change their condition. But once individuals with low confidence understand that they have negative and false beliefs about themselves and their abilities, you can begin to help them create a new belief system and a higher self-confidence.

Another way to view this is to examine the relationship between cognitions, emotions, and behavior. The majority of people who seek the professional help of a psychologist or psychiatrist do so because they want to *feel* differently. The vast majority of these patients suffer from either depression or anxiety, and if you have one, you usually have both.

Between my master's and doctorate degrees, I worked for several years as a psychotherapist. I spent time in both out-patient and in-patient facilities. Teenagers usually ended up in treatment because of their *behavior*. They were not unsatisfied with how they felt, but their parents were certainly unhappy with how they behaved. Adults, on the other hand, usually came to treatment primarily because of how they felt. There were frequently behavioral concerns, but it was emotional distress that initially got them into treatment. Yet, of all the people I treated over those years, I can never remember anyone coming into treatment asking me to help them change the way they thought or to alter their belief system. They wanted to feel and behave differently, but they didn't want to give up the inaccurate belief system that was at the root of their troubles.

Good therapies and most religions both have something in common: the search for the truth. Once the quest for the truth is replaced with a desire to feel good, the journey is over. The search for truth is a cognitive process that requires both the conscious and unconscious mind in order to succeed.

As Dr. Lipton so clearly states, "Beliefs control biology." I would make a small amendment to that. Beliefs control biology, biology controls behavior, and behavior determines success.

KEY TAKEAWAY

In the battle of mind vs. body, mind always wins!

Consider this: What if you suffer from a case of mistaken identity? Who you *think* you are is not actually who you are. What you *think* you are here to do is not actually what you are here to do. What you *think* you are capable of is actually only a hint of your true ability.

Consider for a moment that you are totally wrong about yourself—and wrong about this infinite universe in which you live. What if that's true? What if most of us live our entire lives and never know who we actually are, why we are here, and what we are supposed to do while visiting this planet? What if we have amnesia and forgot who we really are right before we left our mothers' bodies and entered the world? I think this is exactly our state.

Who we think we are is not who we are. We are much, much more than our perceived selves.

The Buddhists have a saying, "Don't mistake the finger pointing to the moon for the moon itself." We think our ego—our persona—is who we really are. But this is only to the same extent that your clothes, your hairstyle and your personality are who you are. In order to reach your full potential—your greatness—you must first admit that you are wrong about yourself.

2

MONK CHARACTER

*If I were dropped out of a plane into the ocean and told the nearest
land was 1,000 miles away, I'd still swim.
And I'd despise the one who gave up.*

– Abraham Maslow

The greatest endurance athletes in the world are not even athletes—they're Buddhist monks living on Mount Hiei in Japan.

For them, there is no competition to win, no competitor to beat, no trophy to hoist, and no lucrative contract to sign. The 1,000 marathons they complete over seven years are viewed as a meditation, not a competition. The goal is personal transformation and enlightenment—not just for themselves, but for others as well.

What they do is amazing, but what they *don't* do is even more incredible.

Sixteen years ago, while watching the 1998 Winter Olympic Games, I was introduced to the Marathon Monks of Mount Hiei (near Kyoto) and have been intrigued by them ever since. For me, theirs is the most amazing story of human achievement ever told.

These monks don't just complete a marathon; they walk/run 1,000 marathons over seven years. To put this in perspective, the monks walk further than the equatorial circumference of earth. They travel 46,572KM—the earth is 40,075KM (or 29,901 miles).

It was one of those things that while you are actually watching it, a part of your brain is telling you that this can't be true—that it's impossible. It was amazing then, and after researching the monks and their lives, it is even more amazing to me now.

As Westerners, we have developed a belief system that suggests to us what is humanly possible and what is not. Our belief system dictates what we believe we are capable of and what we're not; what we should attempt and what we should leave alone.

Our unconscious mind dictates every aspect of our human lives, but what if this system is wrong? What if more is possible than we believe? What if Western science does not have all of the answers regarding human potential? What if our culture, science, and belief system are actually keeping us from reaching our potential and even limiting our performance? Are you willing to change your mind? In order to achieve greatness, you'll have to.

KEY TAKEAWAY

What you believe is the most important thing in the world to you. Your beliefs about what is possible and impossible will dictate your behavior and, ultimately, your success.

The monk's marathons are completed in 100-day cycles. In each of the first three years, the monks spend 100 consecutive days on the 40K marathon course. During years four and five, they complete two 100-day marathons. At year six, the distance increases to 60K (37 miles).

Year seven, the monks complete 100 consecutive days of 84K (52 miles) marathons. This is twice the distance of the marathons run in competitive events in the US and throughout the world (26.2 miles). And finally, for a little cool down during the seventh year, the monks complete 100 days of 40K (24.8 miles) marathons.

The 1,000 Day Mountain Marathon by Year

First Year	100 Days	40K each day
Second Year	100 Days	40K each day
Third Year	100 Days	40K each day
Fourth Year	2 x 100 Days	40K each day
Fifth Year	2 x 100 Days	40K each day

The Great Fast: nine days of no food, water or rest

Sixth Year	100 Days	60K each day
Seventh Year	100 Days	84K each day
	100 Days	40K each day

Sources: Video: Written by Christopher Haden, published by Der Documentary, 2002; John Stevens, *The Marathon Monks of Mount Hiei*

While on the marathon, the monks must follow many rules. Their robe and hat may not be removed. They are not allowed to change or deviate from the course. No stopping is allowed for rest or refreshment, although there is one appointed stop where the monks are allowed to sit during a prayer. All prayers, meditations, and chants must be performed correctly, and absolutely no smoking or drinking is allowed.

Most monks sleep about four to five hours a night during the first few years. However, during longer marathons, the monks are limited to less sleep each night. If for some reason the marathon takes longer than expected, monks may get no sleep at all before having to begin the cycle over again.

Symbolism is present throughout the seven-year challenge. Japanese tradition dictates that one puts his sandals on *outside* of the house. Yet, each morning, the monks put their sandals on *inside* the house, which means they have no intention of returning to their home.

Once they begin the process, the monks commit to completing the first 100 days or they must take their own life. After they have accomplished the first 100 days, the monk can petition to be allowed to complete the entire 1,000-day marathon.

Because their Buddhist religion believes in reincarnation and multiple incarnations for a given soul, they view death differently from those in the Western world. Consequently, their fear of death is non-existent. To ensure their commitment to complete the marathons, the monks carry both a piece of rope (to hang themselves) and a suicide knife. Along the course, there are a number of markers signifying where previous monks have perished along the way to remind them of the severity of their commitment.

> ### KEY TAKEAWAY
>
> The impossible is done by those who are willing to risk it all. Those who risk the most achieve the most.

Each monk must ask his superior for permission to walk-jog the marathon. Therefore, because it is self-initiated, they believe they have no right to complain for any reason. Complaining is viewed as a sign of a weak heart (Read that last sentence again!).

As one monk explained, "The more you suffer, the more pleasure you feel. For us, the fact that there is pain simply means we must discover a way to overcome it. If you find the walk painful, you shouldn't have set out. Pain does not really matter. It is only a symptom of the effort you are putting into the task."

The individual and his accomplishments are not significant. Instead, it is being allowed to continue the tradition that matters most. The monk does not view the marathons as something he is doing for himself. He is doing this for the benefit of others, both past and present. The response the monks have for being allowed to complete the marathon is simply *gratitude*.

Buddhists believe that one of the greatest accomplishments an individual can achieve is to truly know themselves and that there should be no limits to what he or she can and should do to be successful in the attempt to become fully aware.

Adversity and the real possibility of death have a powerful way of introducing one to oneself. In great adversity and challenge, a person sees oneself the clearest. You can fake it when things are going well, but that strategy will surely fail once hope is lost.

KEY TAKEAWAY

Increased self-awareness leads to improved performance. Physical and psychological challenge is essential to one's development because it shows us who we truly are. Seek out difficult experiences while your competitors avoid them.

Hoko zen is a form of walking meditation. The marathon monks view the marathon as a meditation and form of transformation rather than a physical exercise. They believe there are only three basic human desires: food, water, and rest. Therefore, the Great Fast (year five) consists of nine days without the basic human desires.

Though modern science suggests that humans can live only seven days without food or water, by withholding these basic needs, these monks believe they can overcome them. By doing so, they are no longer attached to these desires. (Monks lose about 25 percent of their total body weight during the fast).

From 1885 to 1988, only forty-six men (*gyoja*) have completed the 1,000-day marathon. Two of these spiritual athletes have completed the 1,000-day challenge twice, the most famous being Sakai.

Today, Sakai remains the most well-known and respected of all the marathon monks. However, his path to Mount Hiei is not what you might expect. He reports that when he was a child, he did poorly in school, often failing his exams. As a young man, he was a member of the military and during World War II, he belonged to a unit that used biological weapons to kill large numbers of Chinese.

After the Japanese lost the war, Sakai married a cousin who later committed suicide. His family then opened a noodle shop, which burned down soon thereafter. Sakai became depressed and saw no purpose in his life, so he joined the monks of Mount Hiei with a desire to turn his life around.

"I was lazy and had a good for nothing life," he said.

During his first 1,000-day marathon (Sennichi Kiahogyo), Sakai became exhausted and was certain he was destined to die. Instead of carrying the symbolic coin all gyoja carry, Sakai began to carry the equivalent of several hundred dollars so that whoever found his body could arrange for a proper funeral.

One day, while walking the Kiahogyo in the winter, Sakai was attacked and injured by a wild boar, later developing a very painful infection in his foot. He initially ignored the wound, but his first two toes soon swelled to twice their normal size and turned a deep purple.

Aware of his promise to complete the marathon, he lanced the wound with his suicide knife and thought he might pass out from the pain. Sakai held the knife in front of him so that when he lost consciousness, he would impale himself and end his life.

Fortunately, when he came to, he had fallen to the side and had not stabbed himself with his own knife. Encouraged to still be alive, he got up and continued the 1,000-day challenge.

"I did not know how or why, but I survived. Fate intervened," he said.

Sakai believed that he had accessed a higher power. Learning that the reliance on human strength alone was limiting, he was propelled by a force unknown to most.

Sakai frequently expressed his desire to die while performing the first Kaihogyo. Feeling that he had not yet achieved the discipline he sought to acquire, he began a second tour soon after completing the first. Sakai increased his mileage so that he could complete the practice in six years instead of the normal seven. By the time he finished his second 1,000-day marathon challenge, he was sixty-one. All of this was accomplished on a 1,500 calorie vegetarian diet and with only about three hours of sleep each night.

The typical daily diet of a marathon monk:

1:30 a.m.:	Before beginning the marathon, a bowl of miso soup with tofu
7:00 a.m.:	After completing the marathon, miso soup, a bowl of rice with daikon leaves, and grated daikon with soy sauce
10:00 a.m.:	Herbal tea, honey and lemon water
Noon:	The main meal of the day is a half bowl of rice, noodles, boiled vegetables, tofu with sesame seed oil, fermented soybeans, seaweed, pickles, and a glass of milk
2:30 p.m.:	Potato dumpling
6:00 p.m.:	A bowl of rice and soup

The total caloric intake is approximately 1,500 calories. Modern science suggests the monks must consume at least 2,000 calories in order not to lose weight. Despite this discrepancy, the monks stay strong and healthy throughout the ordeal.

Afterwards, Sakai said, "Human life is like a candle. If it burns out halfway, it does no one any good. I want the flame of my practice to consume my candle completely, letting that light illuminate thousands of places. My practice is to live wholeheartedly, with gratitude and without regret."

Years later in an interview, Sakai shared this advice: "The message I wish to convey is please, live each day as if it were your entire life. If you start something today, finish it today. Tomorrow is another world."

In 2004, a monk named Fujinami completed the marathon under the direction of Sakai. Soon after he finished, he reported, "I feel I have accomplished a job; that is all. I do not know whether I should call it enlightenment or not, but the training has taught me that everyone and everything is equal. A human being is not special, there are no special things."

John Stevens is an American who has studied the marathon monks and spent time with them on Mount Hiei. In his book, *The Marathon Monks of Mount Hiei*, Stevens shares an interesting insight into their lives. The insight gives the rest of us hope in attaining our own lofty, seemingly impossible goals.

He states the monks believe that if you train, no matter what the task, you can accomplish it. The monks believe in bringing out their Buddha nature or spirit, which in turns allows a person to reach his or her full potential. If one does not access his or her divinity, the God within, they will not be able to realize their true self and potential.

This is very similar to what St. Augustine said: "If you are loving and diligent, you may do whatever you desire."

Buddhists believe the root of all suffering is desire, attachment, or self (ego). Eliminating the desire for our situation to be different eliminates the suffering. In other words, they believe that your body hurts not because you just exercised all day, but because you want it to feel differently than it actually does. Accepting the situation allows the suffering to end.

Just as with Catholic monks, the marathon monks renounce material possessions and live on the generosity of their devotees. Many discontinue their relationships with family members in order to focus entirely upon their spiritual lifestyle of meditation and silence.

The monks don't do these things for attention or fame—they do them in isolation. Once you get your ego out of the way (the need to be "special"), you become free and reach your true potential. Doing something for attention or accolades will actually hinder your progress.

For the monks, this is serious business. They believe the process is transforming them and their spiritual being is being magnified as their human form diminishes. Buddhist monks see themselves fundamentally as servants and do this for the benefit of others. Through their commitment, they show us all what our capacity is as human beings.

And once they make a commitment, there is no Plan B. These guys are all in and really live the "do or die" approach to life. We may be tempted to judge this and call it irrational, but there is no shame in dying honorably. And because they believe in reincarnation, to them, the physical death is not permanent.

As a society, we tend to separate our physical, psychological, and spiritual health into different compartments. However, the monks live as if these are all connected; what happens in one area effects the others. In other words, there is a spiritual and psychological component to physical activity. Physical suffering can lead to spiritual enlightenment and greater self-awareness.

As your body becomes stronger, you change psychologically as well. And when you push yourself physically to the edge, this can lead to a spiritual awakening in some people—especially when they feel there is a force outside of themselves assisting them.

The primary lesson from the monks is one of commitment. When you commit to doing something—do it! Don't make excuses. Don't renegotiate. Just do what you said you would do—as if your life depended on it.

If you are really willing to sacrifice yourself in this way, over and over again, you can achieve some amazing things. Most of us tend to hold a little back in reserve, not fully committing to anything. But if you fully commit yourself, the impossible truly becomes possible.

3

THE INTENTION OF *WHY*

Things may come to those who wait,
but only the things left by those who hustle.

– Abraham Lincoln

What is to give light must endure burning.

– Viktor Frankl

There is a great line in *Alice in Wonderland* where Alice and the Cheshire Cat meet at a fork in the road. Alice says to the Cat, "Would you tell me, please, which way I ought to go from here?"

That depends a good deal on where you want to get to," said the Cat.

"I don't much care where," said Alice.

"Then it doesn't matter which way you go," purred the Cat.

"So long as I get somewhere," Alice added as an explanation.

"Oh, you're sure to do that," said the Cat, "if you only walk long enough."

The lesson here is that we need to know where we want to go. You don't have to know *exactly* where, but you better at least know the general direction.

The topic of goal setting has received a lot of attention from sport psychologists, coaches, managers, and anyone else who is trying to get you to do more than you are currently. The primary teaching one hears from these experts is that 1) you must have goals, and 2) they must be specific. Without clear goals, you will fail to succeed.

The next step, they explain, is a process in which you state your goals and write them down. Once you have clearly stated your intended goals, the magic begins and one day, you will have achieved your goals because you *wrote them down.*

I just don't buy it. Sure goals help, and writing them down helps reinforce them, but the fact of the matter is people succeed every day without clearly stated goals. That's because these people have something that is even more important—they have *intention.*

Intention is powerful because it addresses the question of *why?* Why are you getting up early to work out? Why are you staying late at work to check-up on your employees? You can have intention without a clearly defined goal and accomplish great things, but if you have a goal without intention, you'll usually fall well short of your dreams.

Recently, I met with several of my college fraternity brothers to catch up. A number of these guys have been very successful in business and have made quite a bit of money over the years. One of my friends, Greg Jordan, had recently sold his company to a larger company and had agreed to stay on as a manager for a couple of years during the transition.

As a way to create accountability amongst the senior managers, his new boss made everyone attend a conference call on Monday mornings where each manager would tell the group what they planned to do that week to enhance the business.

My friend Greg, who had already started and sold several companies and become quite successful in the process, saw this exercise as both unnecessary and elementary. Finally, it was his turn to report to the group.

"Gentlemen," he said, "this week, I am going to do exactly what I have done every week for the past twenty-five years—go have some fun and make some money." He said nothing more.

Everyone on the call was quiet as tension filled the air. Greg was telling them that you can be successful without having specific goals by possessing a belief in yourself and your ability to make it happen. It's not how most people typically think, but it's how we should if we want to get somewhere worth going.

KEY TAKEAWAY

If you know where you want to go, you will find the way there and your way will likely be a route never taken before. The "what" comes before the "how" and the "why" should come before the "what."

Frequently, I begin conversations with clients by asking them a question regarding goals, "What do you want?" The majority of the time, they are unable to answer. Can YOU? What do *you* want? The Dali Lama says that we all want peace of mind, contentment. I find that interesting because I know quite a few successful people who are not content. They never seem to be totally satisfied, yet they still enjoy their lives. They embrace the challenge and struggle of life. Once one challenge is complete, they go after another, never spending much time basking in the glow of their success.

When you have intention, you don't need a goal. The goal is not about the what and the how, but about the *why*. I call this the "Big Why." If you are setting a goal without understanding the reason for it, then maybe you should reevaluate the goal in general.

My main problem with most goal setting is that we play it way too safe. Most of us find out what we want (a goal) and then lay out the steps necessary to get there. Simple enough, right? Wrong! More often than not, the goals we set are those we are very confident we can reach. Why should that be a bad thing? Because we need to realize that failing to reach the goal is a part of reaching the goal.

Recently, I was speaking to a group of salespeople who were each asked to set a sales goal that they were 100 percent certain they could reach if they put forth a solid effort.

After everyone in the room had completed the task, I then asked them to stay with the same goal, but now rewrite it so that they would only be 90 percent certain they could reach the mark. After a few rumblings, they went to work and rewrote their goals.

"Great!" I said. "You're almost there. Now rewrite the goal so that you are only 80 percent sure you will succeed."

The leader of the group shot me a look as though I might be losing my mind, which is very possible. When they had all finished, I asked them to decide how good they really wanted to be.

"For those of you who are satisfied with keeping your job and maybe getting a modest bonus this year, stop here. But as for the rest of you, let's keep going."

"Okay, now rewrite your goal so that you only have a 70 percent chance of success."

After they completed that round, I asked them again if they wanted to stop or keep going. One salesperson in the middle of the room yelled out, "Hell yes—keep going!"

I walked up to him, took out my wallet and gave him $20.

"That attitude will make you a lot of money," I said. "What about the rest of you? How do you feel? Anyone getting nervous?"

A few hands went up.

"Perfect!" I said. "This is what you want—a goal that will get your full attention. One that will get your adrenaline flowing and make you feel like you are approaching the edge. We are almost finished. Now rewrite your goal so that you only have a 60 percent chance of success and a 40 percent chance of failure. *That's* your goal."

That's how you do it. When you set goals, you gotta go big. Setting a goal that has no chance of failure is a waste of time. It's nothing more than a pep rally.

This past year, I turned fifty and wanted to do something big to mark the occasion. I was working with quite a few distance runners at the time and decided I would run another marathon for my birthday. We had been talking quite a lot about setting big goals and I wanted them all to know that I practiced what I preached—or at least attempted to.

A few weeks into the training, I found myself not very excited about running another marathon. I had become friends with Ian Torrence, an experienced runner who has run over 150 ultra-marathons. (Most ultras are 50K and longer and Ian has run quite a few 100-milers).

I asked Ian what I would have to do to run an ultra and he laid out the commitment I would have to make. Right away, I realized that I could run a 50K and maybe a 50-miler. My motivation and excitement immediately increased.

Upon further study, I came to the conclusion that I had a 90 percent chance of completing another marathon, a 60 percent chance of running the 50K (thirty-one miles), and a 40 percent chance of completing a 50-miler.

The weekend before my birthday, I headed out to my favorite running trail, a one-mile loop, and ran 50K. Friends and family joined me and it was a fun time (and yes, painful). Had I not increased my goal from a marathon to a 50K, I would not have maintained the interest or the motivation to complete the task. So, I introduced a greater risk of failure. Suddenly, the challenge had my attention. It made for a true adventure.

KEY TAKEAWAY

Goals that are not frightening are not worth having.

Every now and then, I hear someone talking about a backup plan, a "Plan B." The backup plan is what you do if the primary plan, Plan A, doesn't work out. When we create a Plan B, it's not so much of a safety net, but a noose. It's a great way to sabotage yourself. Anyone with a Plan B is not totally committed to the Plan A. They are hedging their bets. People with a Plan B are planning to fail—they just don't know it yet. Kill Plan B or it will kill you.

It is absolutely imperative that once you have a plan, you fully commit to that plan. The Plan B agenda will keep you from totally committing and ultimately hinder your performance. Having just one plan and fully committing to it is the best strategy for success.

4

DOING THE IMPOSSIBLE

There are two ways to live: you can live as if nothing is a miracle;
you can live as if everything is a miracle.

– Albert Einstein

Several years ago, I read a biography of St. Francis of Assisi. At the time, I had no idea that a man who died almost eight hundred years before I was born would cause me to leave my home and travel halfway across the world just so I could walk where he walked, sleep where he had slept, and pray where he had prayed.

Because of my schedule, December was the only time I could make the pilgrimage. My Italian friends discouraged me from going in the winter, but I was determined. It took seven days to walk from Rieti to Assisi. It rained almost every day and even sleeted and snowed on me, but I have no regrets. Here's why…

Francis was born in 1182 to a wealthy family in Assisi, Italy. In his early years, he was no different than most of his buddies. He played hard and was the life of the party wherever he went. His desire was to become a knight and be respected for his courage and honor.

During a battle with a neighboring town, Francis was captured and taken prisoner. He remained incarcerated for about a year, malnourished and suffering with malaria, until his family paid a ransom to have him released.

Francis would never be the same. He simply could not go back to living a life that didn't matter.

His eyes were opened and he clearly saw the injustices that he had looked past in his youth. He saw the power and corruption of the church and the lost opportunity that had overtaken an organization that took its constituency for granted.

While praying in the dilapidated chapel of San Damiano, Francis believed he heard God speak to him and the message he heard was clear: "Rebuild my church."

Francis viewed this as his life's mission and went to work rebuilding the church where he had been praying. He would spend the next two years rebuilding three deteriorating chapels near Assisi, though he had no formal training as a builder, no money to buy materials, and no place to sleep. It didn't matter. He was a man on a mission; he pursued his calling with all his heart, mind, and energy.

KEY TAKEAWAY

If you want to live a great life, do what you are capable of, every day.

Reading about St. Francis, one cannot help but be amazed by how much he accomplished, how many lives he affected, and how much influence he had over his generation and those to follow. He became *the* most influential person of his century.

What is even more amazing is that he did this while having no position of power or authority and with only the clothes on his back. Francis voluntarily chose poverty and required all who joined him in the early Franciscan movement to take a vow of poverty also. They were told to sell everything they owned, give the money to the poor, and go live with him.

While still alive, he eventually lost control over the order he founded because he was unwilling to lower his standards and principles. Nevertheless, his ability to accomplish so much in only twenty years made me want to seek out the secret to his success firsthand. Francis did not leave behind much in the way of writings, so it took quite a bit of reading before I finally came across what I believe captures the genius and passion of St. Francis of Assisi:

"First do what is necessary…Then do the possible…And then you will find yourself doing the impossible."

To me, this quote undoubtedly represents how Francis was able to achieve tremendous success and impact so many people.

First do what is necessary.

When you are beginning a task, a day, a job, or even something that feels impossible, just do what you can. That's what *necessary* means. Do the "have to" stuff first; complete your to-do list.

You may spend years of your life just doing the necessary and there is no shame in that. Remember: Francis spent the first two years of his new life gathering and stacking rocks as he rebuilt three chapels.

Master the basics of your craft, business or sport. Focus on the fundamentals. I have made a pretty good living telling people things they already know. I'm just a reminder. Doing the necessary enables you to move to the next stage.

Then do the possible.

Once you have mastered the basics, the fundamentals, it's time to challenge yourself to see what you are truly capable of: the *possible*. Doing the possible is fully within your reach and ability. You are not being asked to become something you are not; you are to simply become all that you already are. The possible requires your full attention, full commitment and unwillingness to go backwards to the safety of necessary.

Most of the people in business today believe that each day they go to work and do their very best, which is the possible. Not true. My observations are that most of us do the necessary and then tell ourselves we are doing the possible.

Think about it: Most of the workforce completes their job requirements—the "to-do" list—and stops there. Have you ever heard someone say, "That's not my job," or "That's not my responsibility," or "I don't get paid to do that?" That's the problem with most of us! We do the *necessary* but call it the *possible*.

You will never perform to your ability if you think the necessary is the possible. The best thing you can do to improve your performance is to think you are doing worse than you actually are, not better.

KEY TAKEAWAY

There is more danger in overestimating your performance than underestimating it.

That's what Francis did. He constantly required more of himself. He neither believed he was doing all that he could, nor thought his Brothers were doing all they could. That's why they eventually ran him off from the organization that he founded. He just wanted everyone to do what they were capable of: the possible.

There is a wonderful story of Francis and his brother walking along a road together. Francis is sharing his regrets and shortcomings and instructs his companion to agree with his self-flagellating comments after he recites his inadequacies.

Instead, his friend disagrees with Francis, assuring him that he really is a good man who has done well. Francis insists and finally his friend agrees to play along and tell Francis what a disappointment and waste his life has been.

Finally, Francis is satisfied that he has done a thorough job of telling himself the unflattering truth and is able to carry on. Believing he had not done enough allowed him to do more.

And then you will find yourself doing the impossible.

The mystery and magic of this lesson comes in this third line. If you are able to commit yourself to doing all that is possible each and every day, a wonderful and marvelous thing will happen to you.

You will find that what you once thought of as impossible, you now view as possible.

In other words, you have the ability to make the impossible possible simply by doing the possible. Notice what changes in this: not the world, but *you*. You transform yourself by doing what is possible, not by doing the necessary.

Remember, we live in a world of people who do the necessary and call it possible. Your vision of the world is changed as you change your behavior and daily disciplines. We have the power to transform ourselves. And when we transform ourselves, we transform others.

When the impossible becomes the possible, you are a different person. The caterpillar has become a butterfly. You will never see yourself the same way, nor will you think of others as you had in the past. Your thoughts and beliefs are altered. What was true is now false—the lie is now the truth.

When the impossible is possible, the world gets smaller and your impact upon it gets bigger. You see that your actions are not separate from what others will do. Duality is gone and unity is now the new reality.

5

THE MYTH OF 110%

There are three musts that hold us back: I must do well.
You must treat me well. And the world must be easy.

– Albert Ellis

There is no 110 percent effort, 100 percent is extremely rare (your best day ever), and 90 percent will guarantee tremendous success.

Most of us love to brag and let the world know just how hard we are working.

The athlete tells us he's giving it 110 percent and the businessman informs us that he works 80 hours a week. We're supposed to be impressed, but I'm not. I feel sorry for them. Although effort is important, it isn't the *most important thing.*

Performance—the result—is what ultimately gets recorded and becomes the metric that you will be measured by. You don't get any extra points for grunting and groaning and making it hard.

While there is a correlation between effort and performance, that correlation is not always positive. Working too hard or putting forth too much effort can actually *decrease* performance. I know of many over-trained athletes and overworked managers who fail to perform well because they are simply exhausted. Their effort is high, performance is low. That's why the 110 percent statement is really nothing to brag about.

It is imperative that each person finds his or her ideal effort level—the level that leads to optimal performance. I can't tell you what yours is, but I guarantee you it's not 110 percent.

When we talk about performing at a high level, there are three considerations: the effort or energy asserted; the condition of the physical body (are you tired, injured, etc.); and your mental state (are you calm, focused, agitated or upset). Together, these three components determine performance.

In our culture, we focus on giving 110 percent effort, but that's more than you actually have. What's interesting is that when you talk to people who have performed at a very high level, they often say it felt easy and at times effortless. They weren't thinking about trying harder or putting forth more effort—their mind was quiet and focused on one thing. They were, as we say, "in the zone." Yes, they are trying, but they are not fighting against themselves and making themselves perform—it naturally happens or it doesn't.

Often, when your effort level is at 80–90 percent, your body is at a 90 percent, and your mind is quiet—you may even feel it's at zero—that's what leads to a high performance.

Here's why.

In competition, you are already putting forth a greater effort because the sympathetic nervous system is aroused. Adrenaline is now in your blood and your body is working harder, putting forth more effort without you consciously trying harder. It's a wonderful thing, but not when you add even more effort to the equation.

The better mental strategy for a competitive environment is to remain relaxed by putting forth a moderate to high effort in the beginning and then increasing your effort if you need to. Research has shown that successful people are both conscientious and possess a moderate level of anxiety about their performance. If you are already successful and trying to get to the next level, adding more effort or stress will not likely be of much help.

Whether you like it or not, you are an expert at self-deception. We all are.

Most people lie about their level of effort and performance and their superiors unfortunately play along with the lie in an attempt to be nice. One hundred percent is all you've got—it's your absolute best effort, all you are capable of. But rarely does a human being invest 100 percent of themselves into any activity, and rarely is their performance optimal if they do.

My estimate is that when most people are really trying, they are giving an effort of between 70–80 percent. Because of this, we have come to believe that 80 percent is our full exertion. On the rare occasion that someone really asserts himself for an extended period of time and moves the needle up to say, 90 percent, he has the sensation of realizing his best and that's when you might hear him say, "I gave it 110 percent."

No, you didn't; one hundred percent is *all you have*, and most great athletes and successful business people hit the 100 percent mark only once every few weeks. If you can sustain an 80 percent effort on a regular basis, you will be extremely successful.

A true "100 percent performance" is not just a complete physical effort. In order for us to maximize our abilities, we must also be in an optimal *mental* state.

What is remarkable about this condition is that the individual does not have an experience of trying hard or fully exerting themselves. In fact, the person may have the sensation of effortlessness while performing at this high level.

Many times, effort is about resistance. I believe we are truly at our best when we accept what is and work with it versus trying to change or stop it. Exerting force against something is quite different than working with the force.

Think of paddling a canoe in a river. You can go with the current or against it. The greatest of us figure out how to go *with* the current, while the rest fight the current and then brag about their 110 percent effort.

When we talk about the zone or flow, the mental state associated with the highest level of performance, we are talking about someone who is not resisting the forces around them, but instead working in concert with them.

Years ago, I was in Pittsburgh for a head injury conference and the Pittsburgh Penguins were in town playing hockey. I decided to head down to the arena and was fortunate enough to get a seat quite close to the action.

Mario Lemieux was playing that night and the fans were excited. Lemieux had serious health problems throughout his career, which had limited his playing time. The previous year, he had to sit out with an uncertain future and had retired the following year, in 1997, only to come out of retirement and play again.

What I observed that night was something I have only witnessed a few times in my life. When Lemieux took possession of the puck, time slowed down. He moved in a way that no one else could. Even though he appeared to be in slow motion, he was not. He was in perfect alignment with the external forces around him. He was going downstream while everyone else seemed to be paddling frantically upstream. It appeared effortless.

This is the thing of legends. When we see them, we instantly know that something about them makes them different. Now we know why.

When we are functioning at a true 100 percent and "in the zone," the conscious mind is quiet and the unconscious mind is in charge. When individuals describe their effort as being at 110 percent, the conscious mind is dominant and they have the experience of exerting *a lot* of effort. This state is usually associated with a performance level of much less than optimal, say about 80 percent.

Convincing high achievers to trust themselves and their trained abilities is a very difficult sale. But when you take your hands off the wheel and give up the illusion of control, that's when the magic happens.

Many of my clients struggle because they are attempting to do a task perfectly. They believe that "perfect" is the only route to success when in fact, attempting to be perfect is a guarantee that you will not perform to your ability.

When I work with someone who is struggling and performing at a level lower than their normal ability, I usually advise them to *lower* their effort when doing the task. I also suggest that they intentionally make a mistake. When they stop trying to be perfect, the conscious mind relaxes and allows the natural ability to surface and an increase in performance is usually the response.

For most people, realizing that less is more comes as a big surprise. They just can't believe it to be true because it is so contrary to what most of us have been taught our entire lives. Instead of focusing on percentages—which are subjective and largely a result of rhetoric and drama—just focus on doing your best.

At the end of each day, ask yourself this question: "Was that the best I could do?"

If you are honest, you will discover that you can rarely answer "yes" to that question. You'll also realize that the best you can do on Monday may be very different from the best you can do on Tuesday. After all, we are humans—not machines. And with this awareness, you will witness significant differences in your effort level and performance over time.

There will soon be a day when the best you can do is get out of bed and get dressed. There will also be a day when you could not make a mistake if you tried. Your stars are aligned and everything is coming to you with minimal effort. *Long-term success is learning how to acknowledge those differences and not struggle too much on a bad day.*

A bad day is only a day, not a life.

KEY TAKEAWAY
No matter who you are or how successful you have become, you will have another bad day. Accept it and move on.

After you have shifted your focus from "perfect" to "best," ask yourself: "Did I get better today? Did I move another step towards my goal, my full potential?"

You should be able to answer yes to that question the majority of your days. Once you focus your attention on getting better each day, begin keeping a written record of your performance. On the days you improved, give yourself a "W" for a win. Days that you fail to advance, give yourself an "L" for a loss.

Once you are able to get Ws about 80–90 percent of the time, you are well on your way to doing something great. Remember: you are not trying to be *the* winner—you are trying to be *a* winner. The greatest men and women are not competing against you; they are competing against themselves each and every day. *You* are your greatest competition. And the next time you hear someone brag about how they gave 110 percent, let that be a reminder of what *not* to do or say.

6

SETTING THE EXPECTATION

The chief danger in life is that you may take too many precautions.

– Alfred Adler

One extends one's limits only by exceeding them.

– M. Scott Peck

I met Barbara Parker and her husband, Sean, in 2007 while working with Pete Rea and the Zap Elite team in Blowing Rock, North Carolina.

At the time, Barbara and Sean were two very good college runners who would later marry after graduating from Florida State University. Barbara is from England and had received a scholarship from FSU to run cross-country, the 1500m, 5000m and the steeplechase.

After a successful collegiate career, Barbara ran professionally with the goal of becoming an Olympian and representing the United Kingdom. In 2008, she made the UK team and ran the steeplechase in Beijing, China. Unfortunately, she failed to advance past the preliminary round.

Though she did not run very well at her first Olympics, Barbara achieved her goal of making the Olympic team. Like most first time

Olympians, her primary goal was to make the team, not win a race or medal.

Many first time Olympians are finished before they even get the chance to compete because they have no real goal or expectation beyond walking in the opening ceremonies. Simply making the team completes the dream. When you ask most first time Olympians how they did, they'll say, "Not well, but that's okay. I just feel so fortunate to have made the team."

Barbara knew she could run faster and continued to train with Sean as her coach. In the summer of 2011, she made the World Championship team that competed in Daegu, South Korea. This time, Barbara ran fast enough to get past the prelims and into the finals by placing in the top fifteen. However, once in the finals, she ran poorly.

Upon retelling the story to me the first time, I asked her what her goal was for the World Championships.

"Get to the finals," she said.

At this point, I suggested to her that she always reaches her goal in these big events.

"No I don't," she fired back.

"Well, think about it, Barbara," I said. "Your goal in 2008 was to make the Olympic team. You did. Your goal at the Worlds was to make the finals. You did."

"Yeah, I made the finals, but I ran terribly and got dropped early in the race," she said.

"But you had no intention of doing anything in that race other than finishing it, and you did that—you finished."

"What do you mean?" she questioned.

"You didn't go into the finals with the intention of placing and you certainly weren't trying to win the damn thing, now were you? You did exactly what you intended to do, nothing more and nothing less."

At that, Barbara looked down, paused a moment and said, "Yeah, I guess you're right."

"So, let me ask you this: what is your goal for the 2012 Olympics?"

Barbara thought for a moment. "I definitely want to make it to the finals. I know I can do it because I made the finals at Worlds. I should make it—I'm one of the fifteen best in the world."

"Every morning, all fifteen women who are going to make the finals in the women's steeplechase get up, put on their running shoes and head out to train—right?" I asked her.

Barbara nodded her head, yes.

"Probably all fifteen of those women expect to make the finals. They all believe they are good enough to make the finals. Would you agree?"

"Sure," she said.

"And how many of those fifteen expect to medal? How many are running today with the intention of winning a medal at the 2012 Olympics in the women's steeple?"

"Oh, I don't know," she said. "There are several Africans who probably think they are going to medal, and the Russian."

"So is it fair to say that every day, some of the women train with the intention of making the team, some train with the expectation of making the finals, some train with the belief that they are going to medal, and a handful train with the goal of winning. Does that sound true to you?"

Barbara agreed.

"So, here we are, eight months away from the Olympics. Let's call it 240 days. You probably have around 200 days of training left, twice a day, for a total of 400 workouts before the Olympics. Who do you think will train hardest? Do you think the women who are training with the hope of making the team will train with the same focus, intensity, and purpose as those who are training to win the gold medal?"

I continued to explain that if she wakes up every day and her whole purpose for living, for existing, for running, is to be the best in the world and to win a gold medal, she has very little in common with someone who would just like to make the team. It's not even close to the same thing.

The runner who expects to win a gold medal has a huge advantage over the rest of the field. Not just at the time of the race, but every day and every training session—and there are 400 training sessions before the Olympics!

If Barbara doesn't expect to win, she has already forfeited the race. And so have you. You have given up your chance to find out just how fast you can go. The best way to approach a race is to win! The only way to find out how good you can really be is to be willing to give everything you have in an attempt to win. The desire to win is the same as the desire to do your best and only those who are trying to win are trying to do their best.

That's why winning is important. It's the path to finding your best.

KEY TAKEAWAY

In order to do your best, you must expect to win.

Barbara, as physically talented as she is, had to be willing to risk everything in order to reach her full potential. That risk included setting a big goal that she might fail to reach.

We revisited her 2012 goals and this time, I asked her what it would take to get on the podium, to medal. "Is there any possible scenario where you can imagine yourself medaling?" I asked.

She thought about it for a while and said, "I have good speed. My last 800 is as fast as anyone's in the world. If I can stay with the lead pack during the first 2000m, I could medal."

"Great! That's your new strategy and goal. So let me ask you, *why* are you running?"

"Because I want to get a medal," she said.

"No, you *expect* to get a medal!"

Everyone wants a medal, but only those who truly believe they will get a medal have a chance. *Wanting* a medal is a conscious desire. *Expecting* to medal is an unconscious belief. There's a big difference between the two. From that day on, we began each session with me asking Barbara again *why* she was still running.

"Because I'm going to win a medal in London," she would say.

"Do you really believe that or are you just telling me what I want to hear?"

"You know, it's really interesting," she said. "At first I had to fake it, but now I am coming to believe that it is true."

In just a few short months, we had gone from trying to get into the finals to expecting to win a medal. Barbara noticed that the intensity and outcome of her training sessions had improved and she would regularly text me with updates.

In order to gauge her progress, Sean would have Barbara repeat certain workouts every few weeks to determine where she needed to improve. Across the board, her attitude towards difficult workouts had changed.

We discussed that if you truly want to get better, then you have to *want* your workouts to be hard, to be painful. It makes no sense to wish away the difficult once you realize that it is essential to your improvement. In order to run a personal best, one must be willing to hurt. If you are wishing away the pain, you are also wishing away the thing that's going to make you better.

One has to learn that pain is the desired state and to not wish it away when it comes.

KEY TAKEAWAY

Expectation dictates performance. Everyone wants to win, but only a very few expect to win.

Winning is never impossible—just look at the sports page of the newspaper. Every day, in every city in America, you can pick up a sports page and read about something that happened the day before that was not supposed to happen.

The best team doesn't always win, even the all-star has a bad night, and the "nobody" can become "somebody." Everyone has a story about the very first time they did something they were never supposed to accomplish. That's the wonder of life—doing the impossible for the first time.

The impossible happens every day in business as well. We just have to understand that these kinds of things don't just happen to other people—they can happen to us as well! But first we must believe that this big crazy miracle called "life" includes each and every one of us.

Remember: Fear is your opponent. No one is better or faster than you—only less afraid.

In June 2012, after five months of training with a winning attitude, Barbara ran the steeplechase in the Prefontaine Classic in Eugene, Oregon. Five of the top seven women in the world were at the starting line.

Prior to this race, we had been working on Barbara taking the risk of going out with the lead runners and establishing herself as one of the runners who expects to medal. During our last session before the race, I suggested she think of herself as a candle. At the beginning of the race, you light the candle. Your goal is to burn the candle all the way down until it begins to flicker.

Then, just as you cross the finish line, take the risk of letting the candle burn out.

It's true—most runners don't want to die during a race. But winning a race is about being *willing* to die during the race. The idea is to preserve nothing and sacrifice everything. That is what "flying" is all about. You have to leave the safety of the ground and take the risk of crashing.

> ## KEY TAKEAWAY
>
> If you want to fly, you must be willing to risk crashing.

Several weeks earlier, Barbara had run in China, but was unable to take the ultimate risk and assert herself at the beginning of the race. It was her first steeplechase race of the season and her confidence was not yet high enough.

Today was different.

It was a strange race from the beginning. For one, the starter's gun wasn't working properly. The women took their places at the line and the gun misfired—false start. They backed-up and waited to take their places at the line again. They lined-up. Another false start.

After the second false start, the television cameras panned from the infield, showing the women—all of whom had stepped back, waiting for the third attempt at a start. Everyone except for Barbara, who stood an entire foot in front of the other women.

Though she was not conscious of it, she was already asserting herself. She felt that she deserved to be in front, deserved to be on the track with the world's best runners. Before the race even began, she was standing out in front of everyone else.

Barbara went out with the leaders and stayed in the lead pack of the race for its entirety. The result was a fourth place finish and a new UK record by five seconds, as well as a personal best.

In the weeks following, we met and reviewed the tape of the race. I showed her where she was standing in front of the other women prior to the start. Barbara had no idea that she was asserting herself before the race had even begun.

That's the power of the unconscious mind—expectation.

7

THE HERO OF YOUR OWN JOURNEY

Courage is being scared to death...and saddling up, anyway.

– John Wayne

Do or do not, there is no try.

– Yoda

Most of the coaches and athletes I work with eventually want to talk about motivation, drive, and goal setting. I don't want to. I hate those topics—they bore the hell out of me and make about as much sense as someone eating a candy bar and washing it down with a Diet Coke.

So, why do they all want to talk about it? Because all of these things—motivation, drive, and goal setting—are really *symptoms*, and we would rather talk about the symptoms than the disease.

Everyone needs a diagnosis, an excuse. *I could be a great runner if it wasn't for this damn asthma; the pain in my knee has really interrupted my training; I have to get my diet figured out.* As long as you have a good excuse as to why you haven't started to fly, you never will.

You've got to get rid of the excuses. They are not your friend and not your path to success. Excuses are the damn boogeyman, stalking you, haunting you, and hiding under your bed so that you pull the covers up over your face.

The real problem is *fear*. Fear is what keeps you from being fully motivated, passionate, driven, and setting big hairy-assed goals. If you had no fear, you would be motivated. If you were fearless, you would be driven and running around with your hair on fire. If you weren't scared, you would be taking over the world and everyone else would get in line behind you.

Fear is your real opponent, not some East African that never owned a pair of shoes until he got a scholarship (your scholarship, I might add) here in the good ole US of A. Fear tells you to slow down because you might get hurt. Fear whispers in your ear, "Are you *sure* this is the right training program? I heard so and so is doing so and so…." Blah, blah, blah.

It's all about fear. If you kill fear, you win. If you kill fear, you have your best year ever. If you kill fear, you train like a mad man. If you kill fear, you go to college for free. If you kill fear, you stand on the podium, you get paid, you have strangers walk up to you and call you by name. When fear dies, you begin to live.

KEY TAKEAWAY

Fear is keeping you from reaching your potential. Conquering fear should be your primary goal in life.

Success over a long period of time is primarily about being singularly focused on one thing—one goal. You have to sell out, and fear is the biggest thing keeping you from selling out.

I thought about writing this book for several years, but I never did it. I had lots of great excuses and used every one of them. Then I noticed I was being followed—stalked by this idea of writing—and it made me really uncomfortable. Every time I would begin to have a peaceful moment, I would think about how I was playing scared, running away from taking the risk of saying what I really thought and putting it out there to be judged.

But the truth is, taking risks and challenging yourself leads to opportunity. Conversely, avoiding risk leads to repetition and mediocrity. Taking a risk and putting it all out there is the best way to achieve something you have not yet accomplished.

The worst advice you can give someone who is trying to be successful is to *be careful*. It decreases creativity and risk taking and deters performance.

KEY TAKEAWAY

"Be careful" is the worst advice you can give someone who is trying to do something great.

In comes the concept of being *chosen* rather than making a choice. I like to think of this as being called. Difficult situations often involve people who are chosen to be in that place at that time.

Take Aron Ralston. Maybe you remember him. He became famous for cutting his arm off rather than dying in a canyon in Utah. When asked in an interview if making the decision to cut off his arm was the most difficult decision of his life, he replied no. Ralston said the most difficult decision he ever made was the decision to quit his lucrative job at Intel and move to Colorado so he could live as an outdoorsman. He knew that family and friends would be critical of his choice to live his dream, versus live the life that was expected of him. After deciding to pursue his passion at all costs, the decisions that followed were not so difficult. Maybe he was called.

The more ego you have, the more fear you have. Ego makes you self-aware, self-conscious, and makes you focus on yourself. Ego makes you wonder and care about what others think about you. The less afraid you become, the less you think about yourself and that allows you to instead think about *what you want.*

What do *you* want? What do you really want? If you could have it any way you please, what would you pick? St. Augustine once said, *Dilige et quod vis fac*; "If you are loving and diligent, you can do whatever you like."

Whatever you like. If you are afraid and undisciplined, which most of us are, you can't do whatever you like because you can't sustain the focus, intention, and energy needed to pull it off.

Do you have something in your life you want badly enough that you are willing to sacrifice everything else in order to achieve it? Keep in mind that if you make this sacrifice, the world will kick your ass. You will be told to "be realistic" or to "think about it" or to "be rational," right? That's the lie that's killing you right now. Greatness is not about being rational and realistic—it's about irrational, crazy thinking.

Chances are that almost everyone you know has given up on themselves and their dreams. So why would they encourage *your* dreams? If you succeed, you will make them more uncomfortable. Average encourages average; mediocre prefers mediocre. In the middle of a competition, there will come a time where you will have the choice to go or not go. I am saying you should *go.*

For most of us, greatness is a threat. Because we haven't achieved it, it's a reminder of what we could-be-but-haven't-yet-become. Greatness is a lonely, dark road in the middle of nowhere. You will run on it all day, all night, and never see another soul. Every now and then, someone will drive by and say, "Hey, what are you doing way the hell out here? You need to get back into town! You can get hurt out here all by yourself! Jump in and I'll give you a ride."

But you have to risk getting lost because chasing a dream—really chasing it—will lead you to places you never thought were out there. Places no one else would ever care (or dare) to go if they knew about them ahead of time.

If you are like most of us, you never want to venture far enough away from home and risk getting lost.

I have a friend, Tyler Winton, who bought an old Harley Davidson motorcycle from me and drove it all over the country one summer. On a long drive from Texas to Georgia, he pulled off the road and went into a service station to get some gas and splash some water on his face.

He asked the woman at the counter, "What town is this?"

She replied, "Honey, are you lost? Where are you trying to get to?"

"No ma'am, I'm not lost.'

"Well, Honey, if you don't know what town you're in, you're lost."

She missed the point. Tyler knew exactly where he was—in the middle of nowhere on a hero's journey, at some no-name exit off I-

20 in Alabama. It doesn't matter where you are, only that you're on your way.

You have to be willing to get lost and wander into unchartered territory. Playing scared keeps you close to the porch and no one ever got lost or broke a world record in their own backyard. Fear keeps you from wandering around and following an unknown path. Greatness is about taking those paths, every day. You have to be willing to go and figure it out. Average will find you, but you have to go out and hunt for greatness.

In *Hero of a Thousand Faces*, Joseph Campbell describes the hero's journey this way: most of us look for a path when we enter a forest. But the hero enters the forest in its deepest and darkest place, where no one has ever entered before. And because he chooses this route, the hero has a very different experience. He faces his demons and the monster that lives in the forest, but when he leaves the forest, he is transformed and changed forever. So you see, the hero is not afraid to get lost, not afraid of the monsters, of failure, and not afraid of death.

Great athletes are on the hero's journey and they are willing to risk their lives in order to complete their journey. This willingness to die—total sacrifice—is critical. However, I'm not suggesting that you become suicidal in order to reach your goals. But if you become truly fearless, then you are afraid of nothing, including death. Not fearing death doesn't mean you want to die. In fact, accepting the simple fact that you will die someday, and that you don't know when that day is coming, helps you to live more fully.

Last month, I spoke to 175 athletes at the University of Arkansas. I asked them, "How many of you would give up two hours a day to become the best athlete in your sport?" All hands went up. Then I asked, "How many of you would be willing to give four hours a day to be the best?" Again all hands went up. That makes sense, because that is the amount of time most college athletes give to their sport each day. Then I asked them, "How many of you would be willing to totally commit your life to becoming the best in the world?" A few hands went up. Shauna Estes-Taylor, the women's golf coach and former coach of the number one female golfer in the world, Stacy Lewis, was sitting on the front row. Shauna and Stacy are close friends and they speak regularly. "Shauna," I asked, "would you say that Stacy has totally committed her life to golf, in order to be the best?"

"Absolutely," said Shauna. Stacy is not the most talented athlete in the world; she was a good player coming out of high school, but was not highly recruited. She had scoliosis and was unable to play her freshman year at Arkansas. It is her heart and fearless commitment to be the best that has allowed her to be the best female golfer in the world.

The people who acknowledge that they have a limited amount of time and live with a sense of urgency have the best chances of living to their full potential. A fear of death is the same as a fear of life. Fear is fear, even though it comes in all shapes and sizes and thirty-one different flavors.

The point I'm trying to make, is that fear keeps you from staying committed to your goal for a long period of time. Think about someone who is trying to make an Olympic team or better yet, win a medal. That is a four-year commitment at least. Keeping focused and passionate for four years is very difficult. Only a small group of people can maintain that level of intensity for that extended period of time.

So how do they do it? Hell if I know. Funny thing is, they don't seem to know either. What they do know is that what they are doing is what they are supposed to be doing. Successful people have a great since of purpose and expectation for their lives. They are on the path of purpose even though they don't truly know where it will lead.

There are a few people who claim to fully understand success, but don't believe a single one of them. You can't follow someone else's path and get there. There is no checklist for success—no map, no GPS, no guarantee, nothing. You have to cut your own path in the woods; fear is the thing that will keep you from doing it.

Just go.

Fear not.

And get yourself lost in your pursuit of success. In your new freedom, you'll find more than you ever thought possible.

8

WHAT DOES FOCUS EVEN MEAN?

The only thing worse than being blind is having sight, but no vision.

– Helen Keller

The word "focus" gets used way too often and most people who tell someone to focus don't even know what they are suggesting.

You can go to any Little League park in the country and in a matter of minutes, some adult will yell at a kid to, "Focus!" *Come on, you guys, you gotta focus!* The kids have no idea what the grown-ups are saying, and neither do the grown-ups.

Or, in business, we frequently hear of poor performers described as lacking or having no focus. *This guy is all over the place, he has no focus and his work product is terrible.*

Focus is a visual concept. It has to do with what you are looking at or what you should be looking at. It is also present tense—it's a *now* concept. Where your eyes are focused is critical to your performance.

In business and in life in general, focus is more about the image one holds in the brain—the mind's eye, if you will. Many spiritual or meditative practices require the person to focus or look at an image or icon for an extended period of time. This leads to a change in the internal state, or certainly that is the intention.

Likewise, looking at a beautiful image or piece of artwork is an act of focus with specific intention. The magic is that as you look at something, what you see changes. Though the object doesn't change, what you see does. The more you focus or look at something, what you are able to see expands and becomes more intricate.

Trained observers see things an untrained observer cannot see. This is quite amazing when you think about it—two people looking at the same thing and seeing two different things, or one not seeing anything at all.

A perfect example of this phenomenon is the ability of an expert in a given field. Let's say, for example, that you are a fairly good golfer with a 12 handicap and you want to get down into the single digits. Your local pro is a great guy, but he's taken you as far as he can. Knowing that you are still unsatisfied with your game, he suggests you go see one of the teachers that several touring pros in the area work with.

You pack your clubs and head out to see the great golf guru. Upon arrival, you are asked to warm up because he wants to see you hit some balls. Before you begin to hit, he sets up five cameras: one in front, one in back, one to your right, one to your left, and one overhead. Every angle is covered. You hit a few balls with a number of different clubs and in a short while, the expert says, "That's enough. Let's go look at the tape."

The pro shows you the tape in real-time speed and comments that you are breaking your wrist at the top of your swing. When you look at the tape in real speed, you can't see what the pro sees. He knows this, so he slows the tape down and sure enough, there it is. At the top of your swing, your wrist breaks and your club head drops, causing a flaw in your swing. He shows you the problem from several other angles until you are convinced that you, too, can see what he sees.

After the video analysis, you are wondering why no one else noticed the problem. The guys you play with are all really good and your pro back home is a scratch golfer. Why didn't anyone pick up on this? The fact of the matter is that they were looking, but didn't *see*. You have to train your eye to see by knowing what and how to focus.

Seeing does you no good if you don't know what to look at. Once the golfer has mastered his swing (of course, no one masters the golf swing for very long), the focus should then remain external. By external, I mean the golfer should then train himself on what to look at.

When I work with golfers, I have them stand on the tee with a driver in hand and look for a directional target. This is usually a tree or some object way off in the distance that the golfer will aim towards. After identifying the target, I ask them to visualize the trajectory of the ball going towards the target.

It is imperative that golfers be able to see the flight of the ball *before* attempting to execute the shot. If you can't imagine it, then you're probably not going to be able to do it. This process of using a directional target is true for all shots that require a full swing.

At some point, depending on the golfer's ability, the aim goes from hitting the ball *towards* the hole to hitting the ball *into* the hole. Focus and target must change in order for this to happen. (Unfortunately, many good golfers never make the mental leap from hitting the ball *towards* to hitting it *in* the hole). Once they are about 100 yards away from the hole and can see the green and flagstick, I ask this question, "Where would the ball need to land in order to go into the hole?"

Surprisingly, most have not thought about holing out from 100–125 yards. But the focus or target changes once you begin trying to hit the ball *in* the hole. Specifically, golfers need to find a spot on the turf that they want to hit with the understanding that if the ball hits that spot, it will go into the hole.

Make no mistake, I am not encouraging the golfer to hit it *near* that spot. I want and expect them to hit *the spot*. If they don't think it's possible, they simply will not be able to do it. Most good golfers are surprised that once they are focused on the spot, they begin to hit the ball very close to the spot and eventually hit the spot.

It's a wonderful thing to observe someone doing something they never thought was possible. After the golfer experiences the magic of focusing on a specific target that is the size of a golf ball, their game is forever changed.

This concept is also true for tennis players. Teaching tennis players to hit the ball to a very specific spot is critical in helping them become more focused and intentional on the court.

Years ago, when my son was playing Little League baseball, I would work with him and some of the other kids in the neighborhood on their hitting. Very rarely will a kid watch the baseball until it hits the bat. However, if you can get a kid to see the ball hit the bat, then they will become a significantly better hitter.

We would spend hours on this simple and basic concept. *Watch the baseball and never take your eye off of it. Watch the ball hit the bat.* I would repeat this over and over again. Most kids follow the ball about three-quarters of the way to the bat but don't follow it all the way. They have to practice this and train their eye to stay focused on the object, not taking their eye off the focal point no matter what. It's easier said than done.

There is no better advice to give a kid learning to hit a ball than to tell them *exactly* what to focus on. The general instruction of "focus" without offering the object to focus on is about as useful as telling a very anxious friend not to worry. It simply doesn't work.

Good coaches and managers understand this and will offer specific instructions that tell the athlete what exactly he or she should be looking at.

For example, in baseball, the batter should be focused on the ball, the pitcher should be focused on the catcher's mitt, and the fielders should be focused on the batter. However, this rarely happens. In fact, it rarely happens at the high school and college levels.

Why? Because no one has ever told the kids *what* exactly they should be focused on. They just keep yelling, "Focus!"

Focus takes practice. People usually understand it, but no one teaches us how. I often do an exercise with athletes to have them think of focus as the beam of a flashlight. You can adjust it to be very large, or you can make it zero in on a particular object. The wide beam is consciousness, while the direct beam is the object of their consciousness. They have to stay tuned in on what that object is. Pretty quickly they readjust their focus.

After you have learned what to focus on with your eyes, you must then know what to focus on with your brain. In golf, they call this a "swing thought."

There is a lot of debate about swing thoughts or, for that matter, any conscious thinking in sport. One could easily argue that the best-case scenario is to have a quiet mind that does not think and has no awareness of itself. I agree, but there are only a small percentage of people who can discipline their minds to that level.

Tempo or timing is of great importance in life and in sport. Everyone has a tempo that allows them to be the most relaxed and natural, thus producing the best result.

Using the mind as a metronome can be extremely helpful. We know that as a person's internal clock speeds up or slows down, performance decreases. You can observe the same phenomena in business. When a person gets anxious, they talk faster and may begin to twitch or move about in an awkward way.

A perfect metronome is our own breath. Our first act of life is to take a breath in, while our last act of life is a breath out. Another tool to focus is a breathing exercise I often use with athletes. I ask them to close their eyes and breathe in while saying the word "in," then breathe out while saying the word "out." Taking the time to focus on this one simple act allows it to translate it to other aspects of their life and sport by creating a steady pace.

Pace is critical and proper focus leads to a steady pace. I often suggest to my clients that they develop a mental approach that will help them stay consistent internally. Continuing with the golf example, I would rather have a golfer count to herself during the swing than say "slow" or "relax." Instead, she should begin her swing with "one," halfway into her backswing is "two," the top of the swing is "three," initiating the downswing is "four," and contact is "five."

It is perfectly fine to alter this cadence, but something similar will work for most golfers. After doing this a few hundred times, the mind unconsciously is set to this tempo and will repeat it automatically. If the athlete gets rattled and loses her tempo, she simply goes back to saying it out loud to herself until she is comfortable with her tempo again.

Focus on your target and then on your intention. A big part of success training involves truly understanding *why* you are doing what you are doing, *how* to do it, and *what* it is you are doing. Focus plays a critical role in this process.

9

FUN EQUALS SUCCESS

Just play. Have fun. Enjoy the game.

– Michael Jordan

Throughout my career, some college coaches have allowed me to come in on a regular basis and meet with their players without the coaches being present. This is a big deal because collegiate coaches are typically very protective of their players and tightly control who has access to them.

I was given access to a baseball team that was into their second season and struggling to find success in their conference, a very competitive league. During one of our weekly meetings, I could see that the tension was very high in the room.

One of the athletes had shared with me during an individual session that the cause of the tension was two-fold: two of the guys were fighting over a girl and the team had lost a couple of close games they should have won. Furthermore, there was a lack of confidence in the coach's ability to help them get past these events.

The meeting began with me asking the team how things were going and what they wanted to discuss during the session. The response was dead silence.

"Anyone have anything they want to say?" I asked. More silence.

I just sat with them in the quiet, knowing that eventually the pressure would build to a point where someone would blow. Finally, one of better athletes blurted out, "This isn't any fun. Playing baseball has been the most fun I've ever had and for the first time, I hate it. I hate coming to practice, I hate the games—I just hate it."

Silence again.

"How about the rest of you?" I asked. "Does anyone else feel the same way?"

Surprisingly, almost all of the hands in the room went up. The men looked around at each other. Finally, one of those who didn't raise his hand said, "But we're not here to have fun. We're here to win games."

"What's the difference?" I asked him. "What's the difference between having fun and winning?"

"I don't understand your question."

I then asked everyone in the room to think of the team they were on when they had the *most* fun playing baseball—any team, any age level. I told them to raise their hands when they had it.

In less than ten seconds, every hand in the room was in the air.

I then went around and I asked each of them to tell me in some detail about that very fun team—how old they were, who they played with, who their coach was, and finally, what their win-loss record was.

The majority of the men told a story of a championship team that had entered each game expecting to win. After five or six told their stories in detail, I asked the group, "Does anyone see a trend developing here?"

"Sure," said the guy who had first started the discussion. "Winning is fun, losing sucks."

"There you go! If you all want to have fun playing baseball, you're going to have to find a way to win. There's nothing fun about public embarrassment, making mistakes and playing below your ability. In a competitive sport, you cannot separate the process from the outcome."

The same is true for almost everything in life. People who enjoy their work have better relationships with colleagues and are more productive than those who don't. Winning will always be fun because winning is associated with playing towards your highest ability. Likewise, losing will always be frustrating because it is associated with fear, lost opportunities, careless errors, and tension.

In business, making money is more enjoyable than losing money. Losing creates intrapersonal tension (anxiety, anger) and interpersonal conflicts (tension between colleagues, talking bad about one another, etc.).

The Gallup organization has conducted some very good research that demonstrates the correlation between the process and outcome at work. They have defined "employee engagement" as the psychological and interpersonal experiences people have at work. Not surprisingly, the research shows that people who have close friends at work, enjoy the tasks they perform, and believe their company's mission is important, are more likely to have a higher rate of production than employees who do not. This higher rate of engagement leads to increased profits for the companies who can create such environments.

Despite the common sense and empirical credibility of such research, we continue to disregard its importance and value. If you like the people you work with and feel that you are well suited for the work you are doing, you will perform at a higher rate than those who don't. Yet, I still hear leaders say, "I don't care if you like me" or "we're not here to have fun—we're here to get the work done."

The truth is, fun and success cannot be separated. Process and outcome are intimately related. You get both or neither.

Don't get me wrong—I like happiness and fun just as much as the next guy. And when things are going my way, I like it. I call that "fun." But be very aware of the fact that the search for fun will not make any of us great. What makes us great is the search for *truth*, and the truth is usually painful.

Seeing yourself as you really are can be humbling and deflating. People who pursue fun are usually willing to tell you (and themselves) a lie in order to keep the fun going. The few who pursue greatness will tell themselves the truth even though it burns down to the bone. They will tell you the truth, too, even if it hurts.

Great managers, coaches, teachers, and parents all have something in common: They will tell you the truth even if it hurts. That's the price we all must pay for greatness. You have to want it to be difficult—even more than you want it to be fun. Do that and the fun (a.k.a. winning) will continue.

KEY TAKEAWAY
The truth may hurt, but never harms.

10

EMBRACING THE TEAM MINDSET

The main ingredient of stardom is the rest of the team.

– John Wooden

Individual commitment to a group effort—
that is what makes a team work, a company work,
a society work, a civilization work.

– Vince Lombardi

I don't believe in such a thing as *individual performance*. Before you get upset, I am quite aware that this is not a popular view in the land of the free and the home of the brave. But regardless, simply stated, no one has ever done anything completely on his or her own.

Of course, there is the illusion of the self-made man: the guy who started work delivering papers when he was a kid, then advanced to stock boy at the local grocery during high school. He put himself through college by working during the day and going to school at night. A wonderful work ethic is developed and he starts his own company after working a couple of years for a larger company just to learn the ropes. Then, twenty years down the road, he is ultra-successful with big money, a large company, and a bigger ego.

When asked about his success, he tells the story of how no one ever gave him a thing and how he worked two jobs to put himself through college. We've all heard this one a hundred times.

But what about the part of the story that never gets told? I want to know how he survived after his birth—how he fed himself and changed his own diapers. Tell me the story about how he taught himself to read (he probably had a great grade-school teacher who cared about him) and how he woke up every morning before sunrise to deliver papers (his neighbor who worked at the paper got him the job). The untold story is always the most interesting one.

We all love a good cowboy movie and we always cheer when the underdog defeats the perennial powerhouse. Yet, at the end of the day, we all need some help to become great. Some need more than others, but we all need help.

KEY TAKEAWAY

No one has ever accomplished anything on his own. There is no such thing as individual performance.

People are successful primarily because they have some innate talent, which they were born with and did nothing to earn; they find themselves in an environment with someone who nurtures their talent and encourages them; and then someone gives them the opportunity to show what they can do.

Throughout the years, I have held hundreds of sessions with individual collegiate athletes. One after another, they would tell me how they performed very well in high school, but now things were not working out so well at college.

Trends began to emerge and I soon realized that if I was ever going to help these athletes, I would need to get them all in a room at the same time. The major problem these elite athletes were having is that they either failed to create a good relationship with the coach or they were at odds with one or more of their teammates.

The commonality for these struggling athletes, I found, was that they had a strong supportive environment back home and had not been able to recreate the positive culture they had enjoyed in high school while at college.

It didn't take much to get them talking. If the team was struggling, I would simply start by asking them why they thought they weren't playing well. After the first person spoke up, the others couldn't wait to get their two cents in.

The teams that were most successful spoke up more easily than the ones that were struggling. I would ask the good teams how good they thought they *could* be.

"Can you all win a conference championship? Can you win the national championship?"

Then I would ask them if they failed to win a championship, what would keep them from going all the way. The issues on higher performing teams were usually more tightly defined and centered around maintaining focus, intensity and the good fortune needed to go long into the playoffs.

But the lower performing teams almost always had either a serious problem with the coach (or coaching staff) or the team had become fractured and sub-teams had established. Certain players would not speak to one another and, after a poor performance, the blame game would begin.

It was always someone else's fault. The anger and frustration were palpable. At times, it was very stressful just to sit in the room with these underperforming teams. However, once the athletes were able to share their hurt and anger without being destructive to one another, the situation would improve and performance would rebound.

I learned that the ideal situation for developing the skills of these athletes was to work with them individually *and* as a group. This model was revised for my corporate clients and as a result, we have developed an outstanding leadership development program.

A sportswriter for the local newspaper at the time had heard that I was working with entire teams and called to ask if he could interview me about the work we were doing. During the interview, I shared with him that the concept of "team"—truly being a unified group—was quite rare in sport and only happens when serious intention and discipline are in place.

I explained that athletes are not going to come together as a unit when they don't know the other people on the team or if they don't trust one another. Furthermore, people work together when they are convinced that they can't obtain the goal without their teammates' help.

If a person thinks he or she can make it alone, they will not collaborate with others.

The process of building a team has several critical components and usually one or more is missing, thus the team never jells and fails to perform at its full potential. Below are the six steps I have found to be critical to teamwork:

Step #1: Recruit and select the right people.

The first step to having a great team is selecting people who are individually talented and who also have the maturity and desire to be a part of something much bigger than themselves. These people have to want to be a member of the team and be willing to adopt the culture and values of the team.

This is the primary role of the coach in sport or the manager in business. The leader must have an eye for talent and be able to differentiate between candidates. If leadership fails during the selection process, there is never a chance for success.

Recently, I was in Dallas, Texas, with a group of VP-level managers who were participating in an experiential leadership program. On this particular day, we visited St. Philips Academy, a private school in one of the worst parts of Dallas.

Crack houses were once located where the school now exists. The director of the school, Dr. Terry Flowers, spoke to our group about his leadership style and how he has been able to defy the odds and create a school that has a 100 percent high school graduation rate in an area where this was once viewed as impossible.

I asked Dr. Flowers what his role was in the selection process for new hires. He quickly responded that he interviews everyone who comes to work in the school. On only a very few occasions, when he had been out of town, had someone been hired without first getting his approval. He added that he generally knows within the first ten minutes if a person will fit into his culture.

I then asked him what he was looking for in a candidate. Without hesitation, he explained that the person must love children in order to join his staff. "If you don't love children, you can't teach them." That was his primary objective: find teachers and staff who love children. After that, the teaching happens automatically.

Step #2: Develop strong friendships.

Once you pick your team, individuals must come to know one another in a fairly intimate way through the sharing of their life stories.

It is imperative that they know about each other's pain and disappointments because they must show vulnerability and take the risk of being rejected for who they truly are. If teammates only share their successes and achievements, trust will never develop. There is no trust without risk and vulnerability.

Step #3: Create a shared belief system.

Everyone must agree on the absolutes of the team—the team rules or mission. This includes what can never happen and what must happen on a regular basis.

There is usually a motto or some unifying belief that everyone holds to be true. Successful teams have a shared belief system. There is a priority—a first and most important thing.

The primary rule is that members are expected to make promises and then keep those promises. Excuses are not tolerated and breaking a promise is a serious offense.

In most of the organizations I consult with, the competition is not another company who provides the same product or service. Instead, the competition is the other managers who work for the same company. When organizations don't work together (and most don't), they compete against one another. It's such a waste and painful to watch.

The movie *A Beautiful Mind* is a true story about John Nash, a brilliant mathematician who also was diagnosed as a paranoid schizophrenic. His greatest achievement was winning the Nobel Prize for Economics with his work on gaming theory. Essentially, he discovered organizations play one of two different types of games: *cooperative games* and strategic or *non-cooperative games.*

The major difference between the two is that in cooperative games, people make and keep their promises to one another. It's referred to as "binding agreements." In strategic games, not only do people *not* make and keep promises to one another, they try to trick and deceive one another in order to win or gain a competitive advantage.

This is what is happening in corporate America today. People who are supposed to be colleagues working for the same good are actually plotting strategically against their own team members. This is best observed between departments or department heads where the turf battle is on display for anyone who cares to pay attention.

Step #4: Fight without hurting each other.

Team members must learn to fight and manage conflict without it becoming destructive.

Conflict is inevitable and the avoidance of conflict only creates more conflict. Teams that try to "play nice" are usually not very successful. Members must value truth-telling as the primary intention when communicating.

It is possible to be honest without being mean or hurtful. Intention is critical in communication and relationship building. With men's teams, we would talk about how they fought with their brothers growing up. The consensus was that while it's okay to cause him pain, you cannot *injure* him.

For the women, we talked about how they fought with their sisters. A similar concept emerged. If you hurt her feelings, you had to apologize afterwards.

Step #5: Cultivate strong leaders.

A successful team must have leadership. The coach must be an effective leader, but there must also be leadership among the athletes or non-managers. Coaches who are unable to groom leaders from within their teams will never be successful.

Unfortunately, most organizations, whether in sport or business, do not have effective leadership. There are people in leadership roles, but they are not leading or inspiring others to reach their full potential. Instead, they tend to just boss their subordinates around.

In my observations, the worst leaders are typically the most senior people in an organization. Usually the best leaders come from two or more levels of management beneath the CEO. Why? Because senior leaders are often out of touch. They don't know their people and their people don't know them. Because of their position, they make the mistake of assuming they are the best leaders in their organizations when they are not.

Step #6: Clearly define the team goal.

Success is clearly defined by a single *team* goal. No individual agendas can be tolerated. The self must be sacrificed in order for the team to excel.

It amazes me how frequently coaches emphasize the success of the team all year long and then have an awards banquet at the end of the year and spend two hours handing out individual trophies like MVP and Most Improved. They believe it encourages and promotes future success, when in reality it does neither.

Business leaders make the same mistake. They, too, profess the benefits of working as a team and achieving group goals, then hand out Employee of the Month awards.

The best leaders create a culture with goals and awards that everyone or no one achieves. Once you create an environment where there are winners and losers at the same time, you will never truly have a team. Everyone must win or no one wins. No exceptions.

Twenty years ago, American culture valued the name on the front of the jersey more than the name on the back. In fact, there was a time when there was no name on the back of the jersey.

In 1929, the Yankees were the first to make numbers a permanent part of the baseball uniform. Numbers were handed out in the order of the line-up (Babe Ruth was #3 because he batted third, Lou Gehrig #4, etc.) The individual was seen primarily as a member of the team. He was valuable only to the extent that he could help his team win.

In the 1960s and 1970s, there was a collective shift in thinking in our society. What used to be a society of "we," became a society of "me." The self-esteem movement began celebrating the individual and it quit being about how much you contributed to the team and instead about individual egos and personalities. Recently, I heard a senior member of the NBA state that the NBA was a league of personalities. He also believed the league should promote the players, not the teams. It's sad to me that most fans come to watch a particular player, not a team.

Today, we value the name on the back of the jersey more than the name on the front and it comes at a high price to the goals of the team. In 2012, the NBA estimated it would make in excess of $100 million in jersey sales that year. At the same time, 22 of the 30 teams were losing money. When the focus is on the individual, athletes and employees cease to play as a team. You simply can't claim the team is most important and at the same time create incentives that suggest the individuals are more valuable than their teams.

In order to be successful, there must be a unified goal. We all win—or lose—together. And the more we win, the harder we work for each other.

11

BELIEFS AND BEHAVIORS

There are three kinds of men: the ones that learn by reading, the few who learn by observation. The rest of them have to pee on the electric fence themselves.

– Will Rogers

It is only when we forget all our learning that we begin to know.

– Henry David Thoreau

Belief is unconscious—it's where what we hold true about ourselves resides. This is also our source of emotion. Though we do not consciously choose our emotional response to events, our emotional response is ultimately dictated by our belief system.

If your emotions are in charge, you will never fully know yourself and you will never reach your potential in a performance environment. That said, the best way to improve your emotional state is to first examine and correct your belief system.

There are three primary components necessary to improve performance: belief, thought, and behavior.

Belief

Beliefs are absolutely critical to performance and ultimately determine how well you will perform. The question is: *Where do our beliefs come from?* How do we come to believe what we hold as truth?

Initially, we all adopt our beliefs from others. For example, during childhood, you probably adopted the beliefs of your parents and other significant people in your life. Think about this for a moment: one of the most important dictators of your performance was not determined by you. Instead, someone else set your life on its current trajectory.

If the people from whom you adopted your self-beliefs did a good and accurate job of telling you the truth about who you really are, consider yourself one of the lucky ones. But what if they were wrong? What if they failed to see your potential, abilities and talents—then what? Well, that's where the problem starts.

We have all adopted some accurate and some inaccurate beliefs. The trouble is, most of us don't know which is which.

> Belief: I am not a good person. My coach doesn't care about me.
>
> Thought: I don't want to be on this team and train today.
>
> Behavior: Poor Performance
>
> Belief: I am a good person. My coach is a good coach.
>
> Thought: I am going to do whatever my coach tells me to do. I trust her.

Behavior: High performance

Thought

Thought is conscious. Our thoughts are usually a byproduct of our beliefs, but it is possible to have a thought that is inconsistent with your beliefs. You can "think" something you don't believe is true.

For example, most people believe there is some aspect about themselves that is not "okay"—something they need to improve about themselves. However, when someone else comments on this particular issue or points out the need for improvement, our unconscious response is typically to become hurt or angry even though we fundamentally agree.

Thought is easier to change than beliefs, so you should therefore put most of your energy towards improving your thinking. Ultimately, you can change your unconscious beliefs through conscious thought.

Behavior

Behavior is what we do. It is very difficult to change behavior long-term, but less difficult to change behavior short-term. Long-term behavior is known as *habit*, while short-term behavior is an *action*. Taking action on a regular basis ultimately leads to a change in habit.

A change to any one of your beliefs, thoughts or behaviors will have an effect on the other two. When all three are aligned, performance is maximized. But most people do not have all three aligned and therefore experience some internal struggle or frustration and their performance is hindered as a result.

How will you know if you are effectively changing your beliefs, thoughts, or behaviors? There is a simple litmus test. You will know when you are changing any one of these because you will be very uncomfortable and may even experience pain during the process. (In fact, more pain is usually associated with greater change and improvement.)

KEY TAKEAWAY

Unfortunately, "No Pain—No Gain" is mostly a true statement.

When we find a bug or error in our belief system, we usually install a "belief patch" to cover up the immediate issue, but we don't typically go back and do the hard work of bringing the entire belief into question. For most of us, that would be way too scary and unsettling.

But if you strive for greatness, that's exactly what you must do. You have to throw the whole thing out and start again from scratch.

Because it is easier to change what we think than it is to change a behavior, we often alter our thoughts rather than change our behavior and habits. Most of us have false beliefs about ourselves that limit our performance and at the same time keep us from making the necessary behavioral changes. Here's an example:

Many athletes believe at some point in their career that they are talented and among the best in their sport at that given level. They believe their talent is the primary reason they are good and that their training habits have a secondary effect on their performance.

The vast majority of really good high school athletes who go on to earn college scholarships fall into this category. They were one of the best kids on their team all through little league and high school. Sure, they trained and practiced hard, but no more than the other athletes they competed with in high school. Eventually, they develop the belief that they can be better than their competitors with the same amount of effort.

Then they go to college, where everyone is talented. They quickly go from being the best athlete on the team to not even playing. They are frequently red-shirted so that they can have another year of development before using up their four years of eligibility. This creates a real problem for most of these athletes and, of course, the same cycle happens again if they make it to the pros.

When most athletes advance to a higher level of play, their beliefs about themselves are usually affected. It's harder to believe you are really good when the talent level increases.

The belief change that the college athlete must make is to begin believing that he or she will be successful—not so much because of physical talent, but because of their work ethic, discipline, knowledge of the game, coachability, and desire to improve. But if they never thought those things were important before, changing their viewpoint is difficult.

This is a condition I refer to as the "curse of talent." The best college athletes change their beliefs about what will make them better once they get to college, while the kids who never change their belief systems never make it in college.

Changing your belief system means you must admit that what you previously believed was wrong or is no longer true. If the belief changes, there can then be a change in behavior. No change in belief equals no change in behavior.

Most of the time when we change our minds, we substitute one false belief for another. This type of belief change does not lead to improvement. But when we substitute a *truth* for a false belief, this does likely lead to an increase in performance.

When belief and thought are not aligned, we call this cognitive dissonance. The lack of alignment causes some internal tension and poor performance. When belief and behavior are not aligned, we will again experience tension. And when thought and behavior are not aligned, again—tension and poor performance.

The ideal scenario—the one that creates the highest level of performance—is when belief, thought and behavior are all aligned. Example: An athlete believes she is talented and has great potential. That is her truth. She thinks, *I am going to work hard to develop my potential because being talented alone will not make me a great competitor.* As a result, she changes her behavior. She goes out every day and works hard.

Learning is basically a relentless pursuit of the truth and this quest will keep you curious and actively engaged throughout your life.

Most great learners are life-long learners. They never stop being curious. As Einstein once described himself, "I have no special talent, I am only passionately curious."

The problem with most performance environments is the assumption that everyone wants to learn, improve, and reach their potential. Unfortunately, this is not the case. What most people want is for you to tell them that everything is okay—that they are fine just the way they are.

This is why you see most people become quite defensive or hurt when someone tells them that they are not performing well or that they need to improve. Those comments disrupt the person's happiness or peace of mind and the belief that they are "doing just fine."

But what about *un-learning*? It is quite possible that un-learning would be much more beneficial to many of us than learning. It has been my observation that the primary barrier to many people's success is all of the stuff they know—their false beliefs—and not necessarily a lack of knowledge.

Think about it: one of the most frustrating experiences we frequently have is dealing with a "know it all." Early in my career, I discovered that many coaches believed they should be a sport psychologist as well as a coach. They pretended to know what they were doing to the detriment of their athletes. The same goes for parents. Have you ever observed an incompetent parent ruin a perfectly good child? I have.

What we have learned, or what we believe is true, is among our greatest hurdles. Some of what you believe is true, really is—but the rest isn't. We just don't know the difference. Ultimately, it's better to *not* know. Not knowing leads to curiosity, where knowing leads to contentment and arrogance—neither of which will increase your performance.

For the small percentage of you who really want to improve and reach your full potential, read on. The rest of you should skip ahead to the next chapter because it's about to get ugly.

Still in? Good! In order to discover the truth about yourself, you must first accept that all humans participate in some level of self-deception. We all lie to ourselves. We do this not because we are bad people, but because we are, well, *people*. There are certain truths about ourselves that are too unsettling to acknowledge, so we massage the truth into a belief that we can live with.

There are also the things that the grown-ups around us tell us about ourselves that are inaccurate, but we believe them anyway. Children are basically trusting and adopt the beliefs of their parents, teachers, and family. But as we said before, they may have gotten it—or at least some of it—wrong. What if, despite all of their good intentions, they simply don't know the truth?

As I explained earlier, social psychology offers a construct called the Looking Glass Phenomena, which basically states that a child looks to his or her immediate surroundings (family, school, etc.) to develop a self-image and other core beliefs.

Are you beginning to see how this can get ugly in a hurry?

As adults who are actively pursuing our full potential, we must go back and revisit all of the things we took at face value as a kid. We must make a list of all of the things we think are true and then ask ourselves, "How do I know this is true? What evidence do I have to demonstrate this truth?"

This is a lengthy and difficult process, but leads to a tremendous amount of insight and discovery. As you work through your list, you will discover that some of your beliefs or truths have little to no supporting data while others do. Yet continue to ask yourself, "What is true and how do I know it is true?"

Once you become comfortable with this process, you will be surprised at what you keep and what you discard. If you are diligent with the exercise, you will find yourself dismissing more "truths" than you keep.

Once you have become proficient at telling yourself the truth, you are then in a place where you can speak candidly and honestly to others. This skill is especially beneficial to people in leadership roles (managers, coaches, parents and teachers). You cannot help a person improve without the ability to speak truthfully.

This means sometimes sharing an opinion or observation that is different from that of others. Differences in opinion often lead to interpersonal tension or crisis, something most people want to avoid. However, it is impossible to improve and develop without a clear sense of what is true and what is not. Each of us has beliefs that benefit us and others that hinder us. We each exhibit behaviors that are both constructive and destructive.

Getting past the desire to be "special" or perfect is absolutely necessary for your growth and improvement. Many of us believe we must be special in order to be okay. If we were to think of ourselves as "average" or "normal," we would become very distraught or depressed.

Believing that you can be normal and also achieve greatness is the truth many of us have yet to realize. Your normality—realizing that you have more in common with others than you are different— is what will allow you to make sense of your struggles and failures.

Essentially, you need to get over yourself. The less time you spend thinking about yourself and the more on what it is you want to do, the better off you will be. Performance increases as one's obsession and concern for self decreases. We don't fail because there is something wrong with us; we fail because we are human.

The human design is not perfect and allows for a lot of variation, thus our performance varies from day to day. Learn to accept this truth and you will be much happier and your overall performance will improve.

Imagine working in an environment where everyone is passionately pursuing the truth about themselves—a place where there is very little ego and quite a bit of humility. These types of environments are almost non-existent. However, this should be our ultimate goal. The best teams and best businesses have this type of environment.

Performance does not take place in a vacuum. All performance is influenced by the environment because humans are social animals. We live in tribes, families, and communities.

When a group of people have become adept at telling themselves the truth, they will automatically begin telling each other the truth. In business environments, we call this feedback. In sport, we call it coaching.

My observation has been that there is very little truth telling in corporate America. In fact, telling the truth is the most dangerous thing one can do in most business and social settings. Most veterans of the corporate world have at least one story of how they went to their boss or colleague, took a risk and shared an honest opinion, and were later penalized for their honesty.

KEY TAKEAWAY

Most people tell lies primary because it is too dangerous to tell the truth—not because of some character defect. Great leaders make it safe for others to tell the truth and then reward that behavior.

Fortunately, leaders of athletic teams are frequently better truth tellers than corporate leaders because there is more objectivity and transparency in sport than business. In sport, you have the concept of *practice*, where it is expected that one will make mistakes while trying to develop a skill or improve.

Business has not yet incorporated the concept of practice into its' milieu. Every meeting and conversation is a game, not practice. Every day is game day.

Now, some business folks may take exception to this concept and say, "We have training programs and that is similar to practice." Well, I'm quite familiar with the training concept in business, which is very similar to our unimpressive educational system. Both corporate and educational systems are very didactic, focusing on reading and listening instead of experimenting and doing. Success is defined by memorizing the right answer and obtaining more knowledge. That system is not effective in bringing about changes in behavior.

Imagine for a minute that you need a surgery that is somewhat complex, but has been performed successfully by a handful of doctors for a couple of years. Now, I want you to pick a surgeon. Here are your choices:

> **Surgeon #1** is a well-respected professor who has written extensively and read everything that has ever been written about your condition and the surgical procedure that you need to have performed, but he has never actually performed the surgery.

> **Surgeon #2** is a practicing surgeon who spends most of her time in the hospital treating patients and performing the surgery that you need. She has

performed the surgery many times and her success rate is high. She does not teach, she does not lecture, and when she gets home she is too tired to read.

Which would you pick? The one with experience, right? In a performance environment, experience is more valuable than information.

Practice allows for failure, even encourages it, if you take the right approach. If you want to create an environment where performance improves, you must first make it safe to fail. That's as true for your individual practices as it is for team practice. Those who are free to admit they fell short can get better. And if you can laugh at yourself when you struggle, feel some discomfort or suffer downright pain, you can get better. Pain is when the real improvement kicks in.

12

THE VALUE OF TIME

Everybody should do at least two things each day
he hates to do, just for practice.

– William James

In my time as a sport psychologist, I have watched a lot of practices. Part of my job is to watch practice and over the years, I have spent a lot of time with the teams I have worked with and watched as many as two to three hours of practice, five times a week. I have observed that practice varies greatly from coach to coach. They value and use time differently and there is a noticeable difference in how they respond to failure and mistakes.

Some coaches know just how to create a high pressured, intense practice environment that simulates competition. Other personalities lead to a more relaxed, focused practice. Still others are experts at creating drills or making the monotony of swimming endless laps interesting.

The best coaches I've seen all have something in common—they understand that the purpose of practice is to prepare for competition. For a competitive athlete, everything—and I mean everything—you do in practice should be to prepare for competition. Great athletes and coaches think about competition during practice; they don't think of practice as separate from competition.

During all of those hours watching practice, I began noticing how time was valued. The best teams utilized their time more efficiently. At the time (and still today), the NCAA had limitations on the amount of time a team could practice each week. Therefore, the better a coach utilized his time, the faster his team would develop. If a drill or activity did not allow the team to perform better in competition, it would be removed and replaced with something that addressed a specific deficit observed during competition.

The teams that didn't succeed also had practices, but they were not organized to maximize time and didn't include the activities the athletes believed were helping them get better.

The great coaches explain *why* certain things are done and the intended outcome of each activity. Once athletes understand why they are doing something, they are better able to fully engage in the activity. When they are not able to understand the purpose of specific activities, they will fail to fully engage in the activity.

KEY TAKEAWAY

Everyone has the same amount of time, but successful people value their time more, thus they are more efficient.

During my first year working at the collegiate level, there was a coach who had not asked me to help with his team. (Ultimately, the coach is the gatekeeper. If he or she didn't want my help, I left them alone). One day I ran into this coach and he asked me to come and watch his practice. I agreed. After watching the first hour, I left to go attend another practice. This went on throughout the week as I watched the first hour of the practice every day that week.

He never talked to me during practice. In fact, he never even acknowledged I was there. I came, I watched, I left. The following week, he called and asked me to come to his office.

"What do you think?" he asked.

"About what?"

"The practice. What did you think about our practice?"

"Coach, I watch a lot of practices and your practices are the quietest practices I have ever seen," I told him. "You are the only one who talks during practice. In fact, I can't even remember hearing your assistant coaches talk."

He seemed surprised by my answer, but I could tell he was thinking about what I had just said. The fact that he had allowed me to come to his practice told me that he had a concern or problem he was unable to solve himself. Yet, he never asked for help. He just wanted my attendance and attention.

"Can I ask you question, coach?"

"Sure. Fire away."

"How would you assess the quality of leadership on your team? Do you have good leadership from any of your players?"

"That's a good question," he said. "I don't think I have *any* leaders on this team and that's one of the things that bothers me."

"Why do you think you don't have any leaders?"

"I'm not sure. I mean, I have some ideas, but I'm not sure. Some of these athletes were really good leaders in high school but they have not stepped up in college."

I asked him if he wanted to hear my thoughts on the subject.

"Yeah," he said. "That's why I asked you watch practice. I didn't want to tell you what the problem was because I thought it would bias your opinion."

"Well Coach, I appreciate you letting me come and watch and yes I do have some thoughts regarding your leadership problem. But I gotta be honest," I said. "I don't think you're going to like me after I tell you what I think is the problem. Are you sure you want me to go on?"

"Hell, yes! Go on. I'm not going to get mad at you. You're trying to help us right?"

"Yeah, that's my intention—to help you. But in order to help you, I have to offend you first." I paused to let him digest that last comment. "The reason you don't have any leaders is because you don't create any space for anyone else to assert themselves. You are the only one who talks in practice. The assistant coaches and all of the athletes are looking to you for what to do next. I have noticed that same thing during your games, too. If you want to have leaders, you gotta allow them to lead. You have to give them some room to step up."

During the run up to the 1996 Olympics, I had the opportunity to watch a couple of Olympians practice over the course of about a year. The Georgia coach had become good friends with a coach in

Cincinnati who had two Olympic gymnastics hopefuls in her gym: Amanda Borden and Jaycee Phelps.

They were both great kids from great families. Not only did Amanda and Jaycee make the 1996 Olympic team, they also won gold medals. It was a great experience for everyone involved.

I had been observing collegiate gymnasts during practice and noticing how individual gymnasts utilized their time. Gymnastics is very different from almost all other sports in that the athlete has a lot of control over how they use their time and what events they focus on in a given practice. My primary focus was calculating how much of an athlete's time was spent training versus the time spent preparing or transitioning between events. Gymnastics is about repetition; whoever gets the most reps in during a practice has a competitive advantage.

What I learned was shocking. The majority of the girls spent less than ten minutes per hour actually training. The remaining time was mostly spent getting prepared or transitioning. At UGA, it was not uncommon to observe a gymnast spending five minutes or less an hour in actual training. And this was one of the best teams in the country at the time and certainly some of the best gymnasts in the country!

I tried this same technique in Cincinnati and saw similar results. Then I observed Amanda Borden utilize twenty minutes in one hour. That was the most productive gymnastics practice session I ever saw. There was a reason she became a gold medalist.

Several years ago, I read Malcom Gladwell's book, *Outliers*, which examines how people achieve greatness. One of the constructs Gladwell believes is necessary for greatness is 10,000 hours of practice. In addition to natural talent and fortunate timing, he proposes that one needs lots of practice in order to achieve greatness.

When I read this, I immediately thought of all the time I had spent watching practices and realized that this had been my observation as well, except that I would add that while a lot of practice was necessary to become great, if that practice was not productive, it would take much longer to reach greatness, if it was ever reached at all. The simple fact is that the more productive, competition-like reps you can get in a practice, the faster you get better.

You have to practice better if you want to get better.

13

A.K.A. LEROY SMITH

You have enemies?
Good. That means you've stood up for something.

– Winston Churchill

When I first began my career as a sport psychologist, I needed to make a little extra money to support my wife and two children.

A small, private liberal arts college with its main campus some fifty miles from Athens decided to open a satellite campus just a few miles away, so I took the opportunity to teach an introductory psychology class there and make a few extra bucks.

After ten years of college and three degrees, I thought I should be able to create an interesting and educational learning experience for my students. It was much harder than I had thought.

Never a fan of teachers who tried to trick or outsmart their students, I took a very direct and straightforward approach to teaching. I lectured on material that was also in the text Monday through Thursday. I had reviews and weekly tests every Friday that together counted for 50 percent of a student's grade for the course.

Every question on the test was included in both the lecture that week and the review that day. Upon completion of the test, students put away their black pens and took out red pens to grade their own tests. Immediately, they knew how they had done. Research has demonstrated that immediate feedback enhances learning; plus, I hated grading papers.

The wildcard for the course was a ten-page research review paper. Students picked their own topics and as long as it was related to psychology, they were allowed to study anything that was of interest to them.

On the first day, I reviewed the syllabus with the class. It clearly stated that papers were due at the beginning of class on their due date. The instructions also stated that late papers would not be accepted and that students would receive a grade of "zero" if their papers were late for any reason.

I explained to the class that part of my job was to prepare them for the real world. One day, they would all (hopefully) have a job and a boss and would be given assignments with deadlines. If they failed to meet the deadline, bad things might happen including possibly being fired.

I wanted them to understand that I was being inflexible, not because I wanted to be mean, but because I wanted them to be prepared for life after college. At the end, I told them it was likely that at least one of them would fail to meet the deadline and would be enraged upon finding out I would not make an exception for them.

Sure enough, on the day the papers were due, one young man failed to appear at the beginning of class. With several minutes remaining, he eventually showed up and took his seat. After class, he approached me and stated that he had completed the paper in plenty of time, but his printer was not working and he had to drive to a copy center to have his paper printed. He handed me the paper and said again how sorry he was that it was late.

"Me too," I said. "This paper is 30 percent of your grade and, unfortunately, you will receive no points for the paper."

He couldn't believe that I wouldn't accept his paper and continued to explain why it was really not a big deal and how it would be okay with him if I wanted to deduct some points for the paper being late.

His protest fell on deaf ears. I suggested he take his case to the dean of the department.

The following day, the dean asked me to stop by his office before class. I did as requested and he very politely told me why my decision was not a good one and how it would be in everyone's best interest if I would accept the student's paper.

I held my ground and suggested we were actually doing the student a favor by helping him learn the importance of a deadline and the value of planning ahead. After several more minutes of discussion, we remained at a stalemate.

I suggested to the dean that if he did not like my decision, he could simply override it by changing the grade I gave the student after I turned in my grades for the quarter. He asked me to grade the paper anyway and submit it to him with my final grades.

I gave the kid an 80 on his paper. It was actually pretty good. But I gave him a zero in the grade book.

I later learned that the dean had taken my grade of 80, subtracted 10 points for tardiness, and given the student credit for the paper. The following semester, I was asked to come back to the school to teach another course. The dean told me that my teacher evaluation scores were very good and that the kids really liked me. I declined. What's the use of being a teacher if you can't teach what really matters most?

Demanding the best from people, holding them accountable, not accepting their excuses, and telling them to do something again are not acts of brutality—they are acts of love. If you truly care about someone, you will run the risk of them becoming angry with you when you do not acquiesce when things get hard.

The best managers and coaches challenge their people. They push them to their limits and create stressful situations so that when difficult times appear they will have been prepared.

There is no success without failure. Success is what you do after you fail. The people in my life who have become great successes have also suffered through quite a few failures. Those who avoid failure or try to help others avoid failure are really just impeding their progress.

I believe we failed in our responsibility to the student who did not turn in his paper on time. Why? Because we did not allow him to fail and learn from his experience. I imagine he went into the workforce and failed to meet other deadlines because he never learned from the pain of failure the first time.

I have a good friend who has been a college professor for many years. He recently told me that parents frequently call him to discuss their child's grade in his class. He stated than when he first started teaching, he never received phone calls from parents. Yet now, it's a regular occurrence, and the parent usually requests that he make a special exception for their child. After all, that's what they have done the child's entire life.

Failure itself is not a bad thing, but repeating the same mistake over and over is a tragedy. There is rarely a time in life when one cannot recover from failure. However, having consecutive failures can be unrecoverable. One of the reasons people have consecutive failures is because they failed to see the value or learn the lesson of the first failure.

Golf is a great example of this truth. Professional golfers will play a poor shot, but almost always use the poor shot to help them refocus and become more intentional in their next shot. Therefore, they rarely hit two bad shots in a row.

Amateur golfers, on the other hand, tend to respond differently to a poor shot. They become angry and lose their ability to focus on the task at hand and are more likely to hit consecutive poor shots—a mistake from which it is almost impossible to recover.

One of the best stories that demonstrates the interconnected relationship of success and failure involves one of the best athletes in history. Michael Jordan was a tenth grader at Laney High school in Wilmington, North Carolina, when he failed to make the varsity basketball team.

The story goes that Michael was only 5'11" at the time, and not yet good enough to play at the varsity level. To make matters worse, one of his tenth grade friends—who was taller and better—did make the varsity team. This failure was so humiliating to Michael that he worked hard to make sure it never happened again.

It was during this time that Michael developed one of the best-known work ethics in all of sport. He was able to take this experience of failure and use it to propel him for years to come. In Jordan's own words, "It all started when Coach Herring cut me.

What it did was instill some values in me. It was a lesson to me to dig within myself."

One can't help but wonder what would have happened if the coach decided not to cut Michael Jordan from the team and let him move up with his friend. There would be no harm in showing a kid some mercy, right? Experiencing success instead of failure could very well have been a curse to Michael and we may have never seen the greatest basketball player of all time had he made varsity his tenth grade year.

To prove my point, anyone know the name of the tenth grader who made the team instead of Michael Jordan? Anyone? His name is Harvest Leroy Smith.

Jordan was so respectful of Smith and the lesson Coach Herring taught him, that he would frequently check into hotels with the alias "Leroy Smith" so as not to alert others that he was coming to town.

Don't feel too bad for Mr. Smith, though. Even though he is not widely known, he did attend the University of North Carolina, Charlotte, on a basketball scholarship and played some pro ball overseas. Smith later became a successful businessman and will always enjoy the satisfaction of knowing he played a key role in the development of one of the greatest athletes of our time.

The common belief is that you become successful by avoiding failure. But this is not true because successful people fail! Success is defined by your response to failure.

When things are not going your way, these challenges or "failures" in life have the capacity to be very informative. They help us create a better awareness of ourselves.

Not only can you not *avoid* failure, you *need* failure to get better. When you fail—and you will—run into it and learn the lesson right away.

14

THE CURSE OF PERFECTION

Do not pray for easy lives. Pray to be stronger men.

– JFK

Do what you can with what you have, where you are.

– Teddy Roosevelt

Most distance runners tend to be very focused, disciplined, and perfectionistic. Their belief is that the desire to be "perfect" will end up making them better. Golfers, gymnasts, placekickers, and baseball pitchers also tend to believe that the desire to be perfect will make them better.

Unfortunately, this is not true most of the time. More often than not, the desire to be perfect actually *hinders* performance. The fact of the matter is that there is no success without failure. How you respond to failure *defines* your success.

Loss and pain are the great motivators to change. Failure leads to change, and change leads to improvement. Not understanding that failure is part of the journey of success will lead to *more* failure— not perfection. Perhaps the best and easiest way to define success is this: fall down 100 times, get up 101.

We must accept that every now and then, we will have a bad day. When I talk with elite athletes, I ask them the following question: "If you were the best athlete in the world in your event, how frequently would you have a bad day?" Surprisingly, many great athletes believe they should get to a point where they no longer have any bad days (failures). But in reality, the best and most self-aware athletes report that during the course of a thirty-day month, they have somewhere between three to six bad days. They understand that it's simply part of the process. The ability to accept these fluctuations in performance allows the athlete to remain fully engaged with their training and keep their goals high. Likewise, the inability to make sense of your failures will ultimately cause you to become discouraged and less motivated and your performance will decline as a result.

How you function during a good day does not define your character. It's how you look during a bad day that is the true test of a man. It is always beneficial for me to see an athlete I am working with have a bad day because it is the truest measure of that person's competitive ability. Do they exacerbate the bad day by becoming even more critical of themselves or someone else? Do they feel sorry for themselves and pout? Do they make excuses and quit? In order for you to reach your potential, you must know how you respond to poor performance. This is critical information you simply cannot move forward without.

So, if perfect is not the goal, what is? It's simple: *Do your best.* That's it. Each and every day, make your intention to do the very best you can that day with what you have that day. As I said earlier, in your daily journal, give yourself a "W" or an "L" for each day. If you did the best you could that day, you get a W. If you did not do your best, you get an L. The goal is to have six or fewer L's in a month. And you never want to have two consecutive L's. It's okay to have a bad day, but you must make yourself recover quickly and get back on track. Remember: the goal is not to be perfect. It's to do your best and recover quickly from failure.

What is perfection?

"Perfection" is a mathematical concept, not a human one. Those who actually achieve perfection, or the human equivalent of perfection, probably aren't trying to be perfect when they in fact bump into the "perfect" moment.

Gymnasts and distance runners have much in common psychologically, as they both tend to be obsessive and have desires to be "perfect." During one practice with a top college gymnastics team in the 1990s, I shared the story of Nadia Comaneci's "perfect" 10.0 during the 1976 Olympics with the girls.

Nadia, a member of the Romanian team, won three gold medals during the 1976 Olympics in Montreal and scored the first perfect 10.0. At age fourteen, she scored a 10.0 on her uneven bars routine. Because it was believed to be impossible to score a perfect 10.0 at that time, the scoreboard could display no score higher than a 9.9. In order to present her score, the officials had to present it as a 1.0. At first the crowd was confused, but they soon figured out that she had in fact scored a perfect 10.0. Nadia went on to score six more perfect 10.0's during her Olympic career.

Most of the gymnasts I was working with were familiar with the story, but were either not born yet or infants during the 1976 Olympics. In their time, perfect 10.0's were quite common in college gymnastics and most of the women on the team were recipients of a 10.0 at some point in their careers. One of the women on the UGA team, Karen Lichey, was regarded as one of the best gymnasts in college at the time and still remains one of the best ever.

The purpose of presenting the Nadia Comaneci story was to address two concepts at once: *perfection* and *impossible*. I shared my thoughts that "perfection" was once paired with "impossible," but now perfection (scoring a 10.0) was commonly viewed as "possible" in college gymnastics. "What's the next impossible thing that will become possible?" I asked the team. We discussed how 200 was the highest possible team score and that no team had ever scored a 200. Additionally, no individual had ever scored a 40 (a perfect 10 on all four events) during a collegiate gymnastics meet. (Though most of the women believed that someone would eventually score a 40 and several had gotten close themselves.)

Later that year, Karen Lichey did the impossible and scored a perfect 40 during a meet. When she and I discussed it during our next session, she shared with me that she had come to realize that a 40 was possible and that she had the ability to pull it off. Karen also shared with me a quote by Walt Disney that our mutual friend, Kirk Smith, had given her before the meet. The Disney quote read: "It's kind of fun to do the impossible."

Sixteen years have passed since Karen Lichey scored the first perfect 40 in women's college gymnastics and since then, no one else has matched her accomplishment. Certainly, many have tried but with no luck. The best advice you could give a gymnast trying to score the next 40 would be, "Don't try to be perfect. Just perform the routine to the best of your ability. Let the judges worry about the score."

Many years ago, I had a client who was an artist. She was a very talented young woman who was quite a poet and a painter, but was frustrated because she was having a block and unable to produce anything that she felt was of value.

In discussing her problem, we realized that the main thing holding her back was her belief that everything had to be perfect in order for her to do her best work. Her stars were not lining up the way she had hoped.

I asked about her belief that everything had to be perfect in order for her to sit down and write. She had assumed that a perfect outcome first required a perfect situation. I suggested that she give up on "perfect" and just work with what she had.

She agreed to write at a certain time each day, no matter what, to see what would happen. Here is what she brought back to our next session:

Don't wait for an invitation, an ideal time, a perfect situation.
It's happening all around you, about you, with or without you.
So, do the do that makes you, you.
Don't wait for another time when you have one available...now.

15

BE...DO...HAVE

It isn't sufficient just to want. You've got to ask yourself what you are going to do to get the things you want.

– Franklin D. Roosevelt

As I've said earlier, when I am working with a new client, I often ask them this simple question: "What do you want?" Surprisingly, most people struggle to come up with an answer.

It's a fairly simple and straightforward question, isn't it? So, answer it right now. Put the book down, get a sheet of paper and write down your answer to the question: *What do you want?*

It's harder than you think, isn't it? Most people struggle to answer this simple question because the fact of the matter is they don't know what they want. Furthermore, they don't think they could have what they wanted even if they knew what they wanted.

When I see a person struggling with the "what do you want?" question, I give them a little help by adding words to the sentence. At this point, I usually draw a pyramid on a sheet of paper or a white board. I then draw two horizontal lines through the pyramid, breaking it into three sections, one on top of the other. I write the word "Have" in the bottom section.

So, let me re-ask you the question this way, "What do you want to have?"

"Oh, now I get it," they respond. "I want to have more money, a bigger house, a new car, a better job…" and off they go like they are sitting on Santa's lap. Everyone has a wish list of things they want and most believe that if they had those things, their life would be better. Next, I write the word "Do" in the middle section of the pyramid.

Let me ask you the question a little differently this time. What do you want to *do*? How do you like to spend your time? What are the activities you enjoy the most?

Most of us are able to answer this question, but some find it harder than the first one. The answers are fewer and there is typically more time between responses. It usually goes something like, "I want to spend more time with my kids, work less, travel more...."

The first question is about material things, stuff. But this question—what do you want to do?—is about how you wish to spend your *time*. What is more valuable to you, your stuff or your time? Be honest. Would you move into a smaller house so you could spend more time with your kids? Would you drive a used car in order to travel to the places you always wanted to go? Unfortunately, most of us value our stuff more than we value our time.

So, how do people who achieve greatness answer these questions? Do they value stuff or time more? That's right, they value time more than money or material goods. But you knew that already...didn't you?

In the top triangle of the pyramid, I write the word "Be." The final question to this trilogy is: What do you want to be? Who am I? It's an important question to be able to answer. But first you must answer, *What am I now?*

Who am I? is the most important and difficult of all questions to answer. When I ask people this question, the vast majority are unable to answer it. *Who am I?* is present tense. *What do I want to be?* is future tense. You have to know who you are now in order to become the person you want to be.

It's kind of like reading a map—in order to figure out how to get somewhere, you have to locate your present position as well as the place you are trying to go. If the first question is about material things, and the second question is about time, the third question is about character. It's about *you*. Remember this is the "Who am I?" question. This question is about telling yourself the truth about who and what you are.

If you have not reached your full potential but want to, then you must first acknowledge that you have not reached your full potential. Understanding the relationship between the "do" and the "be" is imperative and how you spend your time is absolutely critical to what you want to be.

I encourage people to forget about what they want to have or possess—it's a waste of time. Same goes for awards and honors. Forget about that mess. It will not help you improve your performance. Instead, become obsessed with how you spend your time, the choices you make, and who you hang out with. Kids, measure the amount of time you spend working out, reading, doing homework, playing video games. Adults, measure that amount of time you spend at work, in traffic, talking to your kids, waiting at the airport. How you spend your time will dictate what you ultimately become.

My friend and former priest, Paul Winton, once told a group of us, "Show me your checkbook and calendar and I will know who you are." In other words, you can measure a person by how they spend their money and their time. I couldn't agree more.

The consumerism doctrine is that the desire for things leads to the desire for more things. The high performance doctrine is different. It says that the desire for a better use of time leads to a better person. In other words, true desire leads to doing that which leads to a better being.

16

THE SEEKER

*Most people never run far enough on their first wind
to find out they've got a second. Give your dreams all you've
got and you'll be amazed at the energy that comes out of you.*

– William James

Running is physical. Racing is mental.

Have you ever been to a horse race? The energy and excitement of watching these huge animals run so fast is quite dramatic. Yet there is a lot of strategy and planning involved in running and winning a horse race. The favorites usually win, just like with humans, and both have numerous components involved in the outcome.

In horseracing, you have three major components: the horse, the trainer, and the jockey. Horses want to run and they will run to the point of injury if left to their own accord (sounds just like humans). That's where the trainer comes in. The trainer controls almost every aspect of the horse's life: when he runs, how much he runs, how fast he runs, how much he eats, who rides the horse, etc. The jockey is responsible for the horse's behavior while he's on his back.

Before the race, the jockey must be relaxed and confident, which in turn helps the horse to be relaxed. Once the race starts, he must ensure that the horse does not go out too fast and must position the horse on the track so that he will not be encumbered by other horses during the race.

When gamblers go to the track, they assess all three—the horse, the trainer and the jockey—before placing a bet. If one component is missing, the horse will not race well.

Now, let's apply this analogy to humans racing. Your physical body is the equivalent of the horse. Your coach and/or training regimen is the equivalent to the trainer. And your mind or mental state is the jockey. Before the race, you should attend to your physical state and training. But once the race begins, you must be the jockey, not the horse. Your job is to go as fast as you possibly can on that given day.

Training is a physical act. It involves the movement of your body, the conditioning, and the nutrition you have to make your body go. Competing, on the other hand, is primarily a mental activity. It is your ability to use your mind to maximize your body's ability.

What you believe you can do and how you are going to do it all come into play in racing. Great competitors don't run against the competition—they run *with* the competition.

In the Harry Potter movies, Harry plays a most unusual game called Quidditch. The position Harry plays is Seeker. That begs the question, what should we be seeking during competition? The answer is: *the best of ourselves.*

The purpose of competition is to perform at our very best. Great competitors use the competition to help them perform at their best, like a jockey putting his horse in perfect position to win. On the other hand, poor competitors are only inhibited by the competition.

It's amazing how a given situation can bring out the best in one person and the worst in another.

Being a great competitor means that you are able to use the other competitors to help you run fast, not to hinder you. The sole purpose of everyone else in the race is to help you run faster. The person in front of you is simply showing you what is possible. They are saying, "You can do this!"

The desire to win, to be the best in a given moment of time, is a concept that makes many of us uncomfortable. The fact of the matter is, the desire or intention to win will bring out the best in you. You should want to win because it will lead you to your best, not because you will triumph over another.

The world's greatest competitors have a tremendous respect and love for their fellow competitors. They know that they are dependent upon and need the other to do well in order to find the best within themselves. This tension, this struggle, helps create the transformation that great athletes seek. They compete primarily because they desire to be fulfilled, to be complete—not because they wish dominance over another.

In the end, any athlete who competes with the primary desire to be better than someone else—not better than their previous self—will never find their best. It is ultimately you whom you are competing against. It is who-you-are-now versus who-you-could-be.

The Latin root of the word "contest" means, "to testify with or to make a promise with." I love what this suggests. Imagine if every time you entered a contest the promise you made was to do your best. That's all you can do anyway. It is very unsatisfying, and even frustrating to watch a competition in which the athletes did not attempt to do their best. In fact, it is quite a rare thing to see athletes giving it all they have. The majority almost always hold a little something back.

Have you ever driven by a store and seen the sign: "Liquidation Sale—All Items Must Go"? That's what every race should be, a liquidation sale. Everything goes. Everything. When the race is over, you should be empty. Hollow. Spent. Done. Nothing left.

Once you are empty, all that is left is contentment. The only way one can be fully satisfied after a race is to be empty. If you leave anything in reserve, you will be haunted by it until you can race again.

Performing at the highest level is not about talent, ability, size, speed, facilities, equipment, weather conditions, or even effort. It's about being free. Free from expectations of self and others, free from criticism, free from fear, and free from "should" and "have to."

There are many routes to success. Don't be overly invested in a specific outcome or result. This will bite you in the butt every time. Freedom means no attachments, no desire, just one very quiet mind leaving you to perform to the best of your natural abilities that have been trained during intentional practice.

When I talk with an athlete after a great performance, the most common response I hear is no response. They can't tell you what happened or how they did it, it just happened. There is very little memory of the event and time and space tend to be distorted as well. It was absence, not presence, that had allowed the wonderful to happen.

You must trust yourself and your ability in order to perform at that level. Ultimately, you can't will yourself to greatness. But you can trust yourself to greatness if you've done your preparation.

17

PERMISSION TO WIN

A champion is afraid of losing. Everyone else is afraid of winning.

– Billie Jean King

Winning isn't getting ahead of others. It's getting ahead of yourself.

– Roger Staubach

There are two primary drives to win. One is healthy, the other destructive.

Most people want to win so that they can feel better about themselves. If they can associate themselves and their ego with winning, they then come to the conclusion that maybe they are okay after all. And, of course, if they lose, they feel badly because they then must come to the conclusion that something is wrong or broken within them.

This state describes the vast majority of us. The emotional responses to both winning and losing are quite obvious, yet most of us have a stronger response to losing (sadness, frustration, anger) than we do to winning (joy, relief). The competition is an attempt to validate ourselves, to gain approval or recognition from both ourselves and others. We want to win so that we can be "okay."

However, there is a small minority of people who wish to win simply because they want to do their best. They want to experience their "best self" and have learned that in attempting to win, they do their best.

They are not interested in beating you because their desire to win has absolutely nothing to do with you. It is simply their own desire to find out what they can be and do. Therefore, they have no strong emotional response to winning or losing. They realize that nothing is different about them whether they have won or lost. They either learned something about themselves and their ability or they did not. And they are able to quickly make sense of both winning and losing because nothing has changed about who they are.

Growing up in the South, we were always told that there are certain things polite people do not talk about in public. This list includes religion, politics, money, and, of course, sex.

This greatly disappointed me growing up because I thought these were the most interesting things to talk about and that knowing a person's opinions on these subjects was a quick way to see who they truly were. When I got older and became a psychotherapist, I realized that these were also the subjects that tended to cause people the most pain in their lives and their relationships.

In the field of sport and other competitive arenas, there is one topic that tends to get people riled up more than anything else: winning. Early in my career, I wrote a piece about the importance of winning in a newsletter that I sent out to the university's athletic department. Several people, none of whom were coaches, felt the need to visit me at my office to inform me that I was putting out the wrong message by suggesting that winning is important.

I listened to their opinions and thanked them for sharing their concerns, but ultimately concluded that they just didn't get it.

So, here I am again, some twenty years later, about to walk out and stand in front of the firing squad with the same message now validated through two decades of research and experience.

Winning is important, really important.

But not for the reasons you might think.

The winning I'm talking about is not about scoreboards, trophies or championships. It's what happens to a person once he or she has the *desire* to win, the *intention* to win, the *expectation* to win. What I am most interested in is helping people perform at their highest level possible—their full potential. The fact of the matter is that people who have a strong desire to win, to be the best at what they do, are more likely to reach their full potential than someone who says, "I don't care if I win or lose, I just want to get better."

That's why winning matters. It will bring out the best in you and push you to your limits. If winning were more important than getting better, then the best athletes would compete against inferior competition that they knew they could beat when in fact, the best competitors want to compete against the best—even if it means possibly losing.

Frequently, I'll ask a great athlete who is struggling why they don't just play down a level so they can win again. Inevitably, I get the same response: "I would never do that. There's no way I would step down a level so that I could win."

There's the proof that competing against someone who actually has the ability to beat you is more interesting than competing against someone whom you know you can dominate. Sure we want to win, but only if there is joy in winning, which means losing has to be a possibility. And there is only joy if your competition is as good as or better than you are.

One of my many complaints with college football is the scheduling. Because the rating system is subjective and therefore broken, schools have taken to playing down in order to ensure that they have enough wins to make it to a bowl or actually win the national championship. In other words, many schools play two to three games each year against a far inferior opponent in order to pad their schedule with a couple of extra wins. The inferior schools take the game because the payout is significant, up to $1,000,000. Isn't that the definition of prostitution? Doing it for the money, not for the love of the game?

The other problem we have with winning is that we like to put the word "the" before the word "winner," as in, "I am the winner." This terminology suggests that there is only one winner, making everyone else "the loser."

We would be much better off if we put the word "a" before the word "winner," creating the phrase, "I am a winner." This implies that there is more than one winner. The problem we have in our society of narcissism, thin skin, and self-absorption is that everyone is trying to be "the winner" and not "a winner."

Can you and I both be winners? If you are a winner, then must I be a loser? This entire dilemma is created out of insecurity and fear. Let being "the winner" go and start trying to be "a winner." Your level of performance will improve and you will also like yourself a lot more.

I have had the good fortune of working with teams, athletes and companies that cover the full spectrum of the winning-losing continuum. Teams that expect to win practice with a level of intensity that other teams can only wish for. The higher the stakes, the higher the investment by everyone involved.

Imagine going to practice or work every day and knowing that the reason you are doing what you do is because you believe that you and your teammates are going to do something really special, something that history will remember for a long time. Your whole life is changed. There is purpose in everything you do. You matter and everyone else matters, too. It's probably the most fun and excitement an adult human can legally have. That's why winning matters—it escalates the experience to an optimal level.

Another reason winning matters is that winning creates opportunity. In tournament play, winners advance to the next round while the losers go home. In business, winners keep their jobs and make more money, while losers become unemployed or underpaid.

If you enjoy what you do, doing it well allows you to keep doing it, often along new horizons. Success leads to more choices. Positive attributes are placed upon those who succeed at the highest level. I'm not saying this is fair or the way it should be, it's just the way it is.

Employers like to hire candidates who went to prestigious schools or were awarded honors while in college. College coaches prefer an athlete who played for a championship team over one who never played for a winning team. Why? Because we believe that a person who knows how to win, desires to win, and expects to win is a better competitor than one who does not possess those traits. I couldn't agree more.

Years ago, I worked with a team that did not have a history of winning. In fact, they lost more than they won. One day, while meeting with the coach, I asked her how she thought her team would do that year.

"Well, Stan, we are going to try to win every game we play. But, of course, that's not going to happen."

At that point, she lifted up the large calendar on her desk and from under it removed the season's schedule. She described to me how before every season, she would take the schedule and predict whether or not her team would win or lose each of their games.

I was pleased that she would trust me with such private information, but was at the same time surprised by this practice.

"So," I said. "What happens if you win a game you thought you would lose or lose a game you thought you would win? How does this affect your approach to the season?"

It occurred to me that if the coach didn't really think the team would win, it had to affect the way the coach interacted with the team. There's no doubt in my mind that the players know if the coach believes they will win, which is really the same as believing in them as competitors.

The best leaders are the ones who give their organizations the permission to believe that they can win. Teams that win are led by leaders who believe that winning matters and that it's okay to enter into every competition with a positive expectation.

During the course of an athlete's life, there will be times when he or she expects to win and other times when they do not believe they are as good as their competition. Most everyone who reaches the collegiate level of competition has had a point in their career when they wanted to win and believed they would win every time they entered a competition.

However, once they get to the college, Olympic or professional level, this desire and expectation to win usually becomes unstable and less predictable.

One thing I'll do with an athlete who has lost the ability to win is ask them about a time in their career when they expected to and did in fact win. This is not difficult because most of these athletes dominated the competition when they were kids and all the way through high school.

I ask them, "So, what has changed about you? How are you different now? Have you lost your ability? Are you not as good as you once were?"

Immediately, they realize that they are better now than they were in high school and a puzzled look comes over their face. They don't know what happened, but I do. They *lost.*

One day they entered a competition with the same expectation they always had, but this time they got beat and the world has never been the same since. No one ever told them that success is not about avoiding failure but responding to failure.

If winning is important, then competition has to be important as well. In fact, the approach to competition—how you view the competitive environment—is just as important as winning. The process determines the outcome. How you view competition is the process. The final score is the outcome.

In order to do well in a competitive environment, we must learn to focus on the process and not the outcome. Teams that win at a high rate don't talk about winning that much, they talk about how they want to play the game (the process). Great coaches don't try to fire up their teams by screaming, "Let's go out there and win this game!" Rather, they talk about the things they believe the team needs to do in order to win the game.

Believing you are going to win actually gives you permission to not obsess about winning and frees your mind up to focus on the here and now. Believing that you will do well keeps your mind free from distractions and anxious thoughts and a quiet mind leads to a great performance.

KEY TAKEAWAY

Winners don't think about winning. They think about what they must do before a competition to be successful and do very little thinking during the competition itself. Great competitors know when and how to just play the game.

In 1980, Dr. George Sheehan wrote a jewel of a book entitled *This Running Life*. My favorite chapter is a short, three page chapter entitled, "The Spirit." In this chapter, Dr. Sheehan reminds us of the origins of the words "compete" and "contest."

Competition holds the promise to bring out the very best in us and that's why we should seek it out. The word comes from the Latin root *peto*, which means "to go out or to seek." The prefix *com* means "with" or "together." Thus, competition is a social process that requires others. You can't do it by yourself.

But what is it that we should seek during competition? Sheehan suggests we should seek our "absolute best with the help of each other."

I love that statement. It's one of the best sentences I have ever read in my entire life. It captures the notion that we are not in this competitive world alone. We are all here together struggling for the same things.

You want what I want, and I need you in order to achieve my goals. You need me to challenge you so that you can reach your potential. It's poetry.

Great competitors are assisted, not inhibited, by the competition. Going against the best should inspire us, drive us, and set our souls on fire. Competing against the best will bring out the best in you if you learn how to compete *with* and not *against*.

Those who fail to catch the tailwind of competition do so because they compete *against* each other. Great competitors understand the meaning of competing *with* one another.

As we mentioned earlier, *contest* begins with the prefix "con," which also means "with." The second syllable, "test," is the same root as the word "testify."

When we testify, we speak under oath. We make a promise. When we enter a contest, we should make a promise—not only to ourselves, but to everyone present. Sheehan suggests we should promise to do our best.

Whatever you do, make some promise—a commitment—to yourself. Promise you will not quit when it gets difficult. Promise you will not hold anything back. Let the contest be the most important thing in your life at the moment. And make sure you keep your promise to yourself.

People who don't make promises make excuses. Get really good at making and keeping your promises so you won't have to make excuses.

As I mentioned earlier, the problem most people have with winning is that they think there can only be one winner and the rest are losers. Not true. There is no one definition for winning and more than one person can win at a time.

Want an example? Here's a story of how four men won the same race:

It was May 1, 2010, at the Stanford University track. The event was the men's 10,000 meters.

Many of the best distance runners in America show up for the Peyton Jordan Classic and there was a lot of excitement before the race this particular year because Alberto Salazar, the coach of Galen Rupp (the current American record holder) had announced that he believed Rupp would break the American record that night. The hotel ballroom had even been reserved so that Nike could host a big party following this record setting event.

I stood at the fence between two of the best distance coaches in the country: Pete Rea and Greg McMillan. It was magic. The stage was set for the most wonderful of human dramas.

Halfway into the race, the leaders were on record pace and the excitement was building. Everyone watched with Christmas Eve-like anticipation.

With just 600 meters to go, Chris Solinsky—who was known as a 5,000-meter runner and had not been expected to beat Rupp, much less set a new record—took off like he was launched out of a giant slingshot. Rupp and the others took chase and the American record was in serious jeopardy of being broken by not one, but *two* runners.

Solinsky crossed the line in 26:59, shattering Rupp's American record, followed by Rupp in fourth place at 27:10, who also broke the previous record of 27:13. Who won? They both did. They both did exactly what they came to do—set a new American record.

The NCAA record was also rewritten that night by Sam Chelanga of Liberty University with a time of 27:08. And to cap off a wonderful race, the Canadian record was also broken by Simon Bairu, Solinsky's former college teammate, with a time of 27:23.

One race, four new records. In total, thirteen men ran personal bests that evening in the 10,000 meters and all get to tell the story of how they ran in one of the fastest and best 10,000-meter races in the history of track. That night, thirteen men got to say, "I am a winner."

18

THE LUCKY ONES

Winning is not everything, but wanting to win is.

– Vince Lombardi

I frequently hear coaches and athletes refer to an event or result as being either "good luck" or "bad luck." *Luck* is apparently this ethereal mass floating about that either comes to us or abandons us at its own pleasure. Kind of like a muse to an artist, or an angel to a praying child.

It is amazing to me that very accomplished athletes and business people consistently refer to their success as *luck*.

In the book, *Good to Great*, author Jim Collins interviews a number of successful business people and a majority of them state that their tremendous success is due in part to luck or good fortune. What is it, exactly, that they are referring to? Is it possible that when people refer to "luck," they are not talking about the same phenomenon?

I think that's highly likely.

Well, I hate to rain on your parade, but luck is not something that is *out there*, it's *in here*. Sure, luck exists, but only in your mind. It is a creation of your unconscious mind (and sometimes the conscious mind). Basically, it is how you see yourself in relation to the world.

Do you think of yourself as being lucky or unlucky? The truth is, whichever you believe is true is a very big deal. Luck can be your prediction of how you think you are going to perform before an event even begins. In other words, most of us have some premonition of how we will perform before an event starts.

Those who view themselves as lucky believe they will get a break, while the "unlucky" people think the breaks go to others.

Just turn on ESPN on any given day and you will hear your favorite athlete say, "I felt really good in warm ups and I thought tonight might be special, but I had no idea I was going to set a record tonight. I guess I was kinda lucky."

KEY TAKEAWAY

Successful people think of themselves as lucky. They believe the world is working with them, not against them.

Luck can also be used as a form of false humility. In other words, you can say after a successful performance, "We were so much better than our opponent tonight. They're really just not at our level." Or the more common and socially accepted version, "We were just lucky tonight. They are a great team and we feel really fortunate to come out of here with a win." *Really?*

Martin Seligman is a psychologist who has studied optimism (luck) and written quite prolifically about his findings. Seligman suggests that optimism is essentially a belief system that can be learned and has a significant impact upon our lives.

He has discovered that when a particular event happens to us, we automatically attribute this event to either something internal (oneself) or external (the world). We also attribute the outcome to something positive or negative.

As you might imagine, optimistic people attribute positive outcomes to themselves (internal) and negative outcomes to external events.

If you just played really well in a game, for example, you will attempt to make some sense as to why that just happened. An optimist might think, "I played well tonight because I worked hard at practice this week and put forth a great effort during the game" (internal), whereas a pessimist might think, "We won the game tonight because the other team is not very good," or "the referee made a bad call that went our way" (external).

When an optimist has a negative outcome, he or she is more likely to attribute the negative outcome to something external like, "They played really well and all the breaks went their way."

The optimist would not attribute the negative outcome to something internal such as, "I guess I'm just not very good at this." It is imperative that the optimist always preserves his or her sense of well-being by attributing positive outcomes to self and negative outcomes to external factors.

KEY TAKEAWAY

What we refer to as luck is actually what we believe to be true about ourselves and the world. People who have a positive view of themselves and the world are the recipients of good luck.

Take John McEnroe, for example. A number of people have asked me why John McEnroe was such a successful tennis player despite his bad temper and tendency to, at times, come undone.

Sure, McEnroe frequently got mad and lost his temper, but who did McEnroe get mad at? He always got mad at the referee or his opponent (external), but never at himself. McEnroe never became self-critical or angry at himself. His anger was always directed at another and because of this, he was able to maintain a high performance level.

KEY TAKEAWAY

Attribute positive outcomes to your personal traits and abilities. Attribute negative outcomes to external or unusual conditions.

These phenomena of predicting and attributing one's success is nothing new and certainly not found only in sport. A number of my corporate clients have me work with their sales teams and we discuss this topic in great detail.

It usually begins with me asking the group this question: "How many of you have ever had the strong feeling while you were sitting in your car, getting ready to go call on a client, that the sales call was going to go well and that you would make a sale?"

Typically, almost every hand in the room immediately goes up. No one even has to think about their answer—they know before I even finish my question. Of course, being the pain in the butt that I am, I then ask them the reverse.

"Have you ever had a bad feeling in your gut, a sense that the sales call was not going to go well, and that you would be unsuccessful?"

Again, most hands go up, but this time they don't fly up like they did the first time. Instead, a few hands raise, then a few more, and eventually about two-thirds of the group have raised their hands. The remaining one third are either liars or cowards—or maybe a little of both.

This phenomenon can be referred to as "mental handicapping." At your favorite race track, there is a person who has the job of "handicapper." The handicapper's job is to know the horses, jockeys and trainers and make a prediction of what will happen based upon past performances.

The handicapper knows the same things you know—that the past is the best predictor of the future. People don't change much, and neither do horses.

Once someone picks a trajectory, they tend to stay on it. People who have won in the past tend to think they will win in the future. Likewise, the guy who has never won anything has a hard time believing that today is his Lucky Day.

When working with athletes, I ask them what they are preparing for and what they think is going to happen in their competition tomorrow. Commonly, the response is, "I don't know. I hope it goes well." To which I respond, "That's nonsense! You do have an expectation and I want to hear it."

There are then usually a few rounds back and forth of them insisting that they really have no idea. Eventually, they relent and admit that they have been thinking about it quite a bit lately.

I then ask them what they see when they think about the event—what images come to mind. Most admit that the images and thoughts they have are not very positive and because they are so negative, they try to push them back down into their unconscious.

Some people are very good at this form of mental manipulation. However, if you want to be great at your sport, your business or your hobby, you have to get a handle on this. It's huge and it's critical to your future success.

The point is this: when preparing for anything in life, you are engaged in the physical preparation and mental preparation simultaneously. If you are not intentional (conscious) in your mental preparation, you will do it unintentionally or unconsciously.

When the outcome is important, you cannot leave this process to chance, though most of us do. It is not uncommon for an athlete to not even be able to imagine him or herself doing something well or correctly.

I was once asked to assist a college basketball team in improving their free throw percentage. (Interestingly, we had three guys in the top ten of the SEC that year). One player was particularly poor at shooting free throws and, unfortunately, he shot a lot of them.

During one of our first sessions, I asked him to close his eyes and imagine himself shooting the shot. He did and said he missed the shot in that scenario. I explained that this was okay and told him to shoot another. He repeated this exercise a number of times without even being able to imagine himself making a shot.

What this demonstrated was that he thought he was *supposed* to miss the shot, not make it. We would never be able to improve his percentage until we created a mindset where he thought he was supposed to make the shot and thus expected to make the shot each time.

Guys who make more than 80 percent of their free throws generally think that they will make any given single shot. Their self-belief is, "I make my free-throws," or "Free throws are an easy shot."

After working with this athlete for quite some time, he was eventually able to imagine himself making the shot. It was only after this phase that he was able to improve his free throw percentage.

This is a classic example of how one's belief system dictates performance. In order for you to improve, you must change what you believe is true about yourself and your ability.

KEY TAKEAWAY

You always have an expectation of how you will perform. If you are not aware of that expectation then it is probably negative.

When I was at the University of Virginia sitting in on Bob Rotella's graduate seminar class, Rotella was working with quite a few PGA touring pros. One day in class he posed the question, "At the beginning of every PGA event, approximately 150 golfers qualify to play. Of those 150 golfers, how many expect to win the tournament?"

The responses ranged from, "All of them. These are professional golfers," to, "About ten." After all of the responses were in, Rotella shared his. He stated that he did not think more than five to six really believed that they were the one who was supposed to win the tournament.

He outlined the difference between *hoping* to win (which everyone does) from *expecting* to win (which very few do). Essentially, in any competition where there are multiple entrants (golf, tennis, running, swimming, etc.), the majority of the field does not expect to win.

If you don't expect to win, then you have disqualified yourself before the event even begins. You have handicapped yourself out of having a fair chance to win and given the field a head start and unfair advantage.

KEY TAKEAWAY

Your mental goal should be to expect to win or do well at whatever sport or task you participate in.

In June of 2011, a couple of track coaches I had been working with asked me to attend the USA track and field championships in Eugene, Oregon, to work with their athletes.

I flew to Salt Lake City and jumped on a small commuter plane to Eugene. There were quite a few athletes on the flight and I found myself sitting next to one. I figured the young man was a sprinter because one of his thighs was the size of both of mine.

We introduced ourselves and he said he was Justin Gatlin, a sprinter training in Florida. I did not know Justin or that he was a former Olympic gold medalist in the 100m in 2004. Nor was I aware he had won six NCAA titles in two years and left college after his sophomore year to turn pro. Additionally, I was not aware that he had just completed a four-year ban from the sport because his body evidentially produced about as much testosterone as one would normally find at an entire Boy Scout Jamboree. Nevertheless, we got to talking and I shared with him my theory that most runners disqualify themselves before the event even begins because they don't expect to win.

Justin immediately agreed with me and said that in the sprint events, there is usually one—and only one—guy who really thinks he will win. He went so far as to suggest that everyone in the field knows who that person is.

I was quite surprised by his candor and found his description of how sprinters enter a race to be very interesting and informative. We discussed the phenomenon for quite a while and I felt privileged to have one of the greatest sprinters of my time share with me what he truly thought was going on in his mind and in the minds of his competitors.

"Well, Justin, what do you expect will happen to you at this meet?" I quipped.

He said that this was his first meet in quite some time (again, I didn't know he was coming off of a drug suspension) and he would be happy with a top three finish, which would qualify him for the world championships later that year. We said our goodbyes as we exited the plane and I realized then that he would not win the event.

Several days later, I watched the finals with great anticipation. The favorite to win (Tyson Gay) withdrew from the competition due to injury and Justin was now running with a real chance of winning the US championships, something he was not mentally prepared to do.

The gun went off and Justin established himself in the front of the pack and separated as the field soared towards the finish. For a moment, I thought, "Holy shit! He's going to win the race!"

Although his body crossed the finish line first, Justin didn't win. Instead of leaning forward, he looked to his left to see what the competition was doing—a mistake an Olympic champion shouldn't make. Walter Dix won the race in 9.94; Justin came in second with a 9.95

As he looked to his left, Walter Dix leaned forward to win the race and Justin got second. It was his race. He was the fastest guy that day, but unfortunately, I don't think he believed he deserved to win and he surely didn't *expect* to win. If he had, he would have leaned into the tape. Keep in mind, this is an Olympic champion we are talking about. Justin is one of the greatest sprinters ever to compete; he has won hundreds of races.

Think about how crazy this is. The majority of athletes never give themselves a chance to win because they have no expectation of winning or don't believe they deserve to win. If such an athlete was in a position to win a tournament, he or she would almost certainly choke in the end because they find themselves in a position where they do not believe they belong.

We all withdraw to a place of comfort, a position where we think we truly belong. You cannot lie to or fool yourself about how good you really think you are in relationship to your competition. If you don't believe you deserve it, it probably will not happen.

KEY TAKEAWAY

It isn't luck that determines your success—its expectation.

Your expectation is the determinant—not your coach, your mom, or your teammates, but you. It's true that you get what you settle for. Whether you think you are lucky or unlucky, you're right!

19

ONLY ONE WAY TO FAIL

If you're going through Hell, keep going.

– Winston Churchill

This past holiday, a dear family friend visited our family as she had done many times before. Only one thing was different this time, she brought her new boyfriend (let's call him Ken). During our first interactions, I found Ken to be polite, yet very reserved and quiet. After several days into the visit, I learned that Ken was a longtime member of the Army and had been involved with the Special Forces for some time. The Special Forces work very closely with other countries' Special Forces and perform joint operations throughout the world. More recently, their focus has been in Iraq and Afghanistan fighting terrorist groups like Al-Qaeda.

Ken made it quite clear that although it was okay for me to know generally what he did; he could not talk about his work, specifically missions he had been on and ones he was scheduled to participate in the future. However, any idiot with a TV or radio pretty much knows where the hot spots are these days.

After hanging out for the better part of a week, he began to ask me questions about my work as a psychologist and specifically about my thoughts as to why some people perform well in high stress situations while most don't. After hearing my views and evidently accepting them as having some validity, we began talking about the most stressful game of all, WAR. I soon learned that Ken was not only a member of the Special Forces, but he was also a senior ranking officer who was very involved in the selection process as well. We spoke at great length regarding the military's approach to selection and the specific tests they put candidates through to see if they have the temperament to work in the most stressful of all work environments.

Ken described, in detail, a selection exercise that has been used over time with a great deal of success; he smiled the entire time as he shared his observations. The test requires the participants to tread water in a pool about fifteen feet deep. There are quite a few soldiers in the water at one time, and although he wouldn't tell me how many, I got the feeling there were about fifteen to twenty during any one session. The instructions are given to the entire group once, no questions are allowed. Once everyone is in the pool treading water, a whistle is blown. You are to swim to the bottom of the pool, touch the bottom, and swim back up. There are several underwater observers in scuba gear to ensure you touch the bottom and that no one drowns. There will be plenty of opportunity for that later.

Ken developed a wide grin on his face as he described how once all the candidates made it to the top of the water, the whistle was blown again requiring them to go back down after only a quick couple of breaths. Within the first few minutes, candidates would begin to swim to the side of the pool, declaring they either failed to touch the bottom or could not keep up the pace of the exercise. They basically disqualified themselves. Interestingly, there were no instructions given regarding what one should do if he failed to touch the bottom or could not go down when the whistle was blown. The candidates just assumed that if they could not complete the task as described, they were automatically out.

Within five minutes, almost all the candidates would swim to the edge of the pool with a look of frustration and defeat upon their faces. Then Ken said, "The only way one could fail the task was to give up. We design it so that no one can complete the task, but we don't care that you can't complete it. We need men who do not give up when faced with an impossible task." The few that never gave up, never swam over to the side of the pool in defeat, never thought they had failed, were the ones who would ultimately be chosen to be members of this elite group of men.

I found the simplicity of that exercise to be genius and highlighted something I had witnessed over and over again with the athletes I had worked with. Why do some quit while others continue? Why do some assume they have failed when no one told them they had failed? Why do some refuse to believe they have failed when others insist they are a failure? The message is clear, the only way you can fail is to give up. As long as you are trying, treading water, gasping for air, you are succeeding. To fight is to win, to quit is to fail.

This was really juicy stuff and I asked Ken to tell me more about the traits and characteristics they sought.

"One of the things we look for is a person who can turn it on and turn it off."

I was unclear what he meant so I asked a question or two about his statement.

"Stan, a lot of men go into the Army because they want to prove that they are tough and not afraid. They want to kick some ass and then go home and tell their friends and family about all the dangerous things they did. We don't want those guys. We look for guys who don't feel like they need to prove their manhood by taking another life. The guys we choose are not overly proud of what they do or how well they do it. They don't get tattoos or walk around with T-shirts that say what they do. That's what I mean by 'turn it off.' When they are not on an operation, they don't think about it, nor do they want to talk about it either."

Their jobs don't define them and they don't need their job to validate them either. At this point, my friend Ken's girlfriend chimed in. "Stan, I have been around some of the guys he works with and you would never know what they do for a living. They are some of the sweetest, most sincere men I have ever met."

I quickly shared how this is also true with great athletes and great leaders as well. When they are at work, it is the most important thing in the world, but when they leave, they don't think about it very much either. The ability to turn it on and turn it off as Ken defined it, is what allows one to perform at the highest of levels. Turning it off allows one to recover and prepare for the next mission. People who are stressed and unable to recover are the ones who think about their work or sport all the time. They worry and in so doing, deplete their energies and harm their performance. In other words, they have the ability to let whatever they are doing in that moment be the most important thing in their life. This is the essence of focus or concentration. Only one thing matters at a time, and that one thing is the most important thing in the world.

Ken told one last story of a favorite soldier who was on his team. He was also a sniper and well respected by his colleagues. I asked Ken what makes one a great sniper. He answered quickly, "You only take the shot if you are 100 percent sure you can make it. Ninety-nine percent sure and you wait until you get a better shot."

Ken described how lesser marksmen allow themselves to feel rushed and pressured into taking a shot. Not the great ones. They will wait all day for the right second because they realize you must get it right the first time. There are no second chances in that line of work.

Keep in mind, all the snipers have great technical ability. They all can shoot the spots out of aces. It is the ability to manage themselves and their own minds that make them the best.

The sniper was a very warm and gentle guy. Every member has a nickname and his nickname was synonymous with Teddy Bear. Ken told a story about Teddy Bear, where he left out more of the story than he told because it was a classified operation, but here's what I recall.

Their group was about six men and they were in the middle of the bad guys when they realized they were surrounded by the enemy on all sides. There was no way out at the time and they began to acknowledge that this mission was probably not going to end well. While some of the men began to realize that they may be living their last day, Teddy Bear told the group, "They might kill me, but they damn sure are not going to get my chocolate."

He knew that when the enemy killed one of them, they would go through their possessions and take everything they could use. The enemy especially loved chocolate and they all had chocolate bars in their food rations that day. Teddy Bear told all the other soldiers to get the chocolate they had in their packs out and eat it. He said it would be a shame to allow the enemy to not only kill them, but to also eat their chocolate. The team followed his advice and they all began eating the chocolate.

The mood of the team immediately improved. They gained physical energy from the calories and laughed about not letting the enemy eat their chocolate. It was then that they crafted a plan for escaping the enemy and making it out safely without any casualties. Again, another great lesson: No matter how desperate your situation may be, there is always something you can do. You are never a victim; never without a choice. The more difficult the situation, the more challenging it is to recognize what options or choices one has. But remember, you always have a choice.

After the story, I asked Ken how Teddy Bear was able to assert himself as a leader when in fact Ken was the highest ranking officer in the group. "Oh, that doesn't matter to us. Rank doesn't matter on Special Forces teams. In fact, it's expected that you would disagree with anyone if you think their idea is not the best one. That's how we stay alive; we take the best idea no matter who it's from."

Ken went on to say that this was not the case in the normal Army. Rank and power are very much adhered to and soldiers learn early on that they must follow orders. As a general rule, the senior officers have the most experience and are usually correct in the commands they give their troops.

In Special Forces, the rules change. They know that everyone on a Special Forces team is there for a reason; every person has a specific expertise that the others depend upon. Therefore, depending on the issue or situation, the leader or expert changes within the group. Every member is expected to lead and follow, and know when it's their time to lead or follow. Challenging each other is critical to success and survival.

Being with Ken and discussing the topics that we both loved was wonderful. I learned a lot from him and he confirmed some beliefs I had about performance that I developed watching athletes and business people.

When it was time to go, he stuck out his hand and I said I wanted to give him a hug. He had no problem with that; in fact, he gave me a kiss on the cheek as well. It had been a long time since another man had given me a kiss. Perhaps those who are closest to death are also able to live more passionately and freely.

KEY TAKEAWAY

There are an infinite number of ways to become successful, but there is only one way to become a failure—quit.

EPILOGUE

To laugh often and much;
to win the respect of intelligent people and the affection of children;
to earn the appreciation of honest critics and
endure the betrayal of false friends;
to appreciate beauty;
to find the best in others;
to leave the world a bit better, whether by a healthy child,
a garden patch or a redeemed social condition;
to know even one life has breathed easier because you have lived.
This is to have succeeded.

– Ralph Waldo Emerson

I used to believe that I was in control of my life—that there was free will. Now, I believe there is the illusion of control, which is not the same thing as actually being in control. Once our eyes open to this reality, we then get in touch with the better part of ourselves— our souls, the non-physical self. We realize we are motivated not to make more money, win a championship or win the affection of others. We are compelled to be who we are, the best of ourselves. That means conquering our old self. This is when we begin to take flight. This is the time in our lives when we gather up wax and feathers and begin constructing our own wings. We realize we are imprisoned in a world that is no longer acceptable. We can see the other side and believe risking everything, even our lives, is the only thing to do.

Once you are infected with this truth, it will cause you as much pain and suffering as joy. Your family and friends will want to know what's wrong, are you okay? "Don't worry," they will say, "you are just going through a tough time, it will get better." They believe this because they have accepted their prison cell and want you to accept yours—that way it's easier for everyone.

When we have doubt—everyone does despite ability—we benefit from having an encouraging voice in our lives. Without these encouragers, we are all likely to quit or give up on ourselves. When you are able to be an encourager for yourself, you will also be able to do this for others. If you can't be an advocate for yourself, you will likely fail in your attempts to help others.

These are the times when we have no choice or option. In these times, we do not have the luxury of a decision, it is a *have* to. For me, writing this book became a have to. Whether I wanted to or not, this book was going to be written. At first, I tried to escape the responsibility, but just like a ghost it haunted me until I could no longer avoid the inevitable. My unconscious mind would wake me up at 2:30, 3:15, or 4:20. I had two choices: lay in bed awake or get up and write. It was the damnedest thing. Until then, I never believed in possession, but sure enough, it happened to me. Some spirit had entered my soul and I became a possessed man…Shit.

After a few days I learned to quit fighting the spirit that had possessed me and agreed to just go with it…If you can't beat 'em, join 'em, kinda thing. Soon, all I had to do was turn on my laptop and just sit there attentively as the words appeared in my head and my fingers magically typed out the thoughts the spirit was speaking to me. This must be what the artists call a muse. In generations before our time, the word *genius* was not used to describe a person, but something that had entered into a person. The Genius was not us, but some sort of spirit that came from a higher place and temporarily took up residence in one of us. That's what was happening to me. As crazy as it sounds, I didn't write this book, but somehow I will get either the credit or blame for it.

This is one of those experiences that we think is supposed to happen to someone else, someone special. So how could this happen to me? It's simple, it was my time. And be assured, your time is coming. You will not get to pick your time, it will pick you, but your time will definitely come. If you try to hide from it like I did, it will haunt you, wake you up in the middle of the night, speak to you, whisper to you, harass you until you finally say, "Okay, I'll do it."

I'm not sure what you will be picked to do. It probably won't be to write a book, but you will be picked. Maybe you will be chosen to take a job, or run a marathon. Perhaps your calling is to have a child, or adopt one. Some of you will be called to travel to a distant land and meet a stranger. You might join an army and fight for a cause that today you could care less about. But sooner or later it will be your turn...you will be Called. And *please, please, please...do not try to avoid it...you cannot avoid the call.* Just play along with it, it will win. If you fight it, you will lose.

The people who I have referenced in this book all got such a call. We think that those who achieved greatness did so by their own hard work and dedication. That may be true but it is not the whole story. They were picked and decided to play along with whatever it is out there that does the picking. I don't know who or what does the picking, but I can assure you it is not us. It is bigger and more powerful than a human being. It is omniscient and omnipotent. Achieving excellence is one part human participation, but the other part is some kind of divine intervention that I am yet to fully understand. It is these types of questions that make me believe that life really is worth living, despite all the pain and gnashing of teeth we must go through.

After writing the book, I began to have serious doubts about the quality and potential benefit the book would produce. You can call it a "crisis of confidence." Scotty, my editor, regularly told me that the book was coming along well and that it was going to be good. Finally, I got mad at her and said, "Quit being nice to me and telling me how good the book is, I need you to be objective." In her own defense, she reminded me that in addition to writing a number of articles and books, she had read several thousand and had the wisdom and experience to know what is and what isn't a good book. I had to agree with her; that was a pretty objective statement. So, I got up, dusted myself off, and kept going.

After we had finished a first round of edits, we decided that we should send the book out to about five people whom I respect and who could give us some feedback. One of the people I chose to send the draft to was Alicia Shay. I had met Alicia very serendipitously in Flagstaff, Arizona a couple of months earlier. Alicia had run track and cross-country at Stanford University. During her time at Stanford, she had won two NCAA cross-country championships. She also held the NCAA record for the 10,000-meter run. She and her husband Ryan, moved to Flagstaff to continue training. Unfortunately, the couple made national news when Ryan, a very accomplished distance runner, died while competing in the 2008 Olympic marathon trials in New York City. During mile four of the race, Ryan collapsed from a cardiac disorder and never regained consciousness. When Alicia arrived at the hospital, she quickly realized that her husband had not fallen and injured his head like she had been told, but that he was dead from cardiac failure.

When I met her, it was more than four years later. I had just given a talk to a group of adult runners and two elite women runners were in the audience. One of the women, Alvina Begay, I knew and had worked with in the past. The other was Alicia, but we did not know each other at the time. Alvina was giving me a ride back to my hotel and so I waited for her to finish talking with Alicia. We were introduced and Alicia asked if she could contact me in the future. She liked my talk and had a few things she would like to talk with me about. I said sure, and when I offered to give her my number, she told me she had already gotten it from Alvina.

When we got in the car, Alvina said, "Do you know who that was?"

When I replied that I didn't, Alvina began to tell me Alicia's story. Soon, I realized that even though I did not know Alicia, I knew her story. Everyone in America who is a distance runner or works with distance runners knows the story of Ryan Shay and the tragedy of this death. I had just met his widow.

It took less than thirty minutes for Alicia to reach out to me by text and thank me for the talk and say she hoped we could talk sometime. I immediately called her back and told her I was leaving at ten a.m. the next day, but if she would like, we could meet at seven a.m. the following morning. We met for two hours and Alicia told me the story of her life and her desire to get healthy and once again become an elite distant runner.

Back to the book. I emailed Alicia and asked if she'd had a chance to look at the manuscript I sent her. Here is her email response:

Yes! This is incredible. I still have thirty pages left because I keep going back and reading pages, paragraphs and sections over. I'll stop doing that so I can finish quickly! :)

All I can say is WOW! I am so thankful that you put this all down in print. You almost lost me at butterflies and caterpillars (I deleted that piece) but each chapter is so rich and spot on. I'm not just blowing steam. I call things pretty straight and honest.

By the way. I think that I mentioned last time we spoke that the residual issues with my hip seemed to be clearing up...so I want to step on the gas pedal and aim to run NYC (Marathon). I have 8 weeks and I started work outs last week. It is definitely about ½ the amount of time I would like to have for my first marathon build up but I need to start somewhere and this could be a really great opportunity! My physio (therapist) is on board and my coach is coming around to the idea if I can train consistently the next four weeks.

Do you have any thoughts?

I hope your week is going well! Alicia

P.S. Is your daughter still dropping minute PR's with her compression socks? :)

I immediately picked up the phone and called Alicia. Usually I do not get an answer when I try to call her because she lives out in the sticks and does not have good reception. However, this time she answered the phone. I thanked her for reading the book and again asked if she thought I should move forward with trying to get published. "You have to publish this book, Stan. You have to."

Immediately, tears started to flow down my face. I had made a promise to myself that if one person benefited from the book, it would have been worth it. I was getting that confirmation now. It had been worth all that I went through. I succeeded. The book did what I hoped it would do…help one person. And of all the athletes in the world that I would want to help, Alicia Shay would be my first choice.

After getting the validation I needed, we began to talk about Alicia's goal of running the New York City Marathon. Keep in mind, this is the site where her husband had died five years earlier. The last time she ran in New York City was when she ran through the streets of the crowded city in her street clothes to the hospital after being told Ryan had fallen during the marathon trials. The last time she ran in New York City she was thinking about her husband and hoping to find him just a little bruised and bloody. This time it would be Alicia running the marathon. She would be the one risking everything to pursue her dream. It took five years, but now Alicia was ready to put her life on the line. It had all come full circle; it was time for closure.

Just as I had needed her confirmation and encouragement for my book, Alicia was asking for my opinion regarding her plan to run the marathon. We talked about what she thought she could run, how she would approach the race, how she would measure success, and what she hoped to accomplish by running the marathon. It was clear to me that she was ready. "Alicia, I am going to give you the same advice you gave me about the book."

"What's that?" she asked.

"Do you remember what you told me when I asked you if you thought I should publish the book?"

"That you have to?"

"Yes, you said I have to publish the book. And you have to run this marathon. You have to."

Sometimes life gives you choices…other times you just have to.

In a world full of people, there's so few that can fly…I thank God for the few who dare to fly.

These then are my last words to you.
Be not afraid of life.
Believe that life is worth living and
your belief will help create the fact.

— William James

ABOUT THE AUTHOR

 Dr. Stan Beecham is a Sport Psychologist and Leadership Consultant based in Roswell, Georgia. Legendary Coach Vince Dooley gave Beecham his start as an undergraduate student at UGA allowing him to work with Kevin Butler, the great college and professional kicker for the Chicago Bears.

Dooley later hired Dr. Beecham to start the Sport Psychology Program for the Athletic Department. He was instrumental in helping UGA win numerous individual and team championships during his tenure.

Today his work with collegiate, Olympic, and Professional athletes from many sports has afforded him an insight into the minds of great competitors that only few have had the good fortune to gain.

Dr. Beecham has taken his wisdom into the business world as he develops and conducts leadership development programs for corporate clients.

A world-class speaker and presenter, Dr. Beecham shares his vast knowledge and experience in this incredible work.

TO CONTACT THE AUTHOR

www.DrStanBeecham.com